TEACHER to TEACHER

TEACHER

A Music Educator's Survival Guide

Teacher to Teacher

Teacher to Teacher

A Music Educator's
Survival Guide

MENC MENC *The National Association for*
100
1907 - 2007 **MUSIC EDUCATION**

Published in partnership with
MENC: The National Association for Music Education
Frances S. Ponick, Executive Editor

Rowman & Littlefield Education
Lanham • New York • Toronto • Plymouth, UK

Published in partnership with
MENC: The National Association for Music Education

Published in the United States of America
by Rowman & Littlefield Education
A Division of Rowman & Littlefield Publishers, Inc.
A wholly owned subsidary of The Rowman & Littlefield Publishing Group, Inc.
4501 Forbes Boulevard, Suite 200, Lanham, Maryland 20706
www.rowmaneducation.com

Estover Road
Plymouth PL6 7PY
United Kingdom

First Rowman & Littlefield Education edition 2007

British Library Cataloguing in Publication Information Available

Library of Congress Control Number: 2007920986

ISBN-13: 978-1-56545-161-2 (pbk. : alk. paper)
ISBN-10: 1-56545-161-9 (pbk. : alk. paper)

∞™ The paper used in this publication meets the minimum requirements of
American National Standard for Information Sciences—Permanence of
Paper for Printed Library Materials, ANSI/NISO Z39.48-1992.
Manufactured in the United States of America.

Contents

Preface 7

"What'll I Do?" The Daily Challenge of Teaching Music

Introduction by Barbara W. Baker 11

1. What Do I Teach? 13

2. How Do I Teach All This? 27

"I Will Survive" Classroom Management

Introduction by Moe Turrentine 43

3. How Can I Get the Students to Behave?. 45

4. How Can I Stay Organized?. 53

"Heart and Soul" Life Beyond the Classroom

Introduction by Scott D. Laird 61

5. What Personal Characteristics Do I Need?. 63

6. What If I Don't Know Enough? 73

7. How Can I Stay Musical?. 83

8. How Can I Take Care of My Needs?. 93

"People" Personal Relationships

Introduction by Brett Smith 101

9. How Can I Build Better Relationships with My Students? 103

10. How Can I Get Help from My Colleagues?. 115

11. How Can I Build Community Support?. 125

Appendix: MENC Survey Results 134

Contributors 139

Preface

n 2001, MENC: The National Association for Music Education asked its members to participate in an online survey that asked, "What are the essential practices of successful music teachers?" Over 850 teachers responded to this survey, which is described in more detail in the Appendix. These responses provided MENC with a treasure trove of ideas and suggestions that teachers have successfully used in the classroom. This book is a sampling of those survey responses.

As you page through this book, you will see that each chapter opens with a question related to music teaching. Each chapter is organized into a series of short responses to the question that opens the chapter, followed by some of the "best practices" that teachers provided in response to the MENC survey. Though many readers will no doubt benefit from reading this book from beginning to end, it is intended to also serve as a book just for browsing through or consulting for a few fresh ideas or new perspectives. If you do choose to read the book from beginning to end, you may find some overlap between ideas in different sections and some ideas in one chapter that could easily fit into a chapter on another topic altogether.

The sidebars included in each chapter provide specific ideas to inspire you to try something new in your classroom. They include details on techniques that teachers have used to build support for their programs, maintain order in the classroom, and help students grow musically. Lists of books, Web sites, and other resources are also provided.

Because these practices come from many different teachers and because every teacher and teaching situation is unique, you may find some ideas that contradict each other. Music teachers face a variety of challenges, and what works in one classroom for one teacher may be entirely inappropriate in another situation. You know your own situation best and can best determine what will work for you. An idea that could never work in your situation could still inspire you to come up with something new that will work. This is your guide to use as you best see fit. Write in the margins, add your own new ideas, and try something new.

It is our hope that you will enjoy perusing this book, whether you spend a weekend reading it cover to cover or snatch a few minutes here and there to get some tips on a specific topic. Many of the teachers who responded to the essential practices survey commented on how easy it is

Key to Sidebars

Each chapter in this book is filled with sidebars that offer ideas that have worked for music teachers, lists of places where you can look for more information, and suggestions specifically related to certain specialties. Each sidebar is marked with a symbol to help you find the information that interests you the most.

 SUCCESS STORIES: Teachers share stories of specific tricks of the trade that worked for them. Most of these ideas can be used in all sorts of music classrooms.

 LEARN MORE: If you want to learn more about a specific topic, check out some of the resources listed in these sidebars.

 JUST FOR INSTRUMENTALISTS: These ideas are geared toward band and orchestra teachers.

 JUST FOR CHOIR: These ideas are geared toward choir teachers.

 JUST FOR GENERAL MUSIC: These ideas are geared toward general music teachers.

for music teachers to become isolated and what a challenge it is to find opportunities to "shoot the breeze" with other music teachers. This book is intended to be just one small way to help solve that problem. You can continue the discussion by using this book as a springboard for discussion with colleagues, mentors, and community members. Visit the MENC Network Communities at http://www.menc.org/channels.html to explore other ideas. If you are an MENC member, you can join the discussion yourself by posing a question or offering advice. Take advantage of whatever opportunities you have to be in community with other music teachers, and "You'll Never Walk Alone."

1

"What'll I Do?"

The Daily Challenge of Teaching Music

Many of us got into teaching because we had a great role model. That teacher probably had wisdom, experience, and excitement about teaching music. The ideas in this section will remind you of your favorite music teacher, the one who had forgotten more great teaching strategies and ideas than we will ever know. Luckily for us, outstanding teachers responded to this survey with great ideas and real-world wisdom, experience, and excitement.

This section presents great ideas for vocal, general, and instrumental music teachers at every level of experience. I was delighted by the breadth of innovative ideas about teaching every aspect of music to the "whole child." I especially enjoyed the thoughtfulness of the teachers who teach the "tried and true" with a new twist. Many of the ideas suggest students should "do" music (create, sight-read, play loud, move to music, experience world musics), rather than be passive observers of music. They encourage students to make music a permanent part of their lives, whether as music professionals or as casual listeners. These teachers are helping to redefine the role of music in our children's lives as they teach the next generation of performers, teachers, and consumers.

Dr. Barbara W. Baker
Vocal Music Teacher, Music Department
    Chair
Eleanor Roosevelt High School
Greenbelt, Maryland

CHAPTER 1

What Do I Teach?

T he answer to the question that opens this chapter seems obvious enough—you're supposed teach music, of course. But any music teacher knows that the real answer is much more complicated than that. Do you teach students to play and sing music, to compose their own music, to listen to music with appreciation? What is the role of theory? Music history? What type of music should students be singing, playing, and listening to? What about performances? And how does interdisciplinary education fit in?

This chapter offers teachers' insights into their role as music teachers. Teachers share their thoughts about what aspects of music learning are most important in their classrooms.

Put music first.

- First and foremost, deliver the best music possible for and with students—music that can grow and be reinvented.

- I believe it is vitally important to immerse myself and my students in the world of music.

- Teach music—*not performance!* Be sure to base your program on sound musical teaching rather than show business. Music education does imply performance, but not at the expense of either music or education.

- I'm a choir teacher, and we're not here *just* to sing. I want my students to understand what the music means and how it's made. I believe it's important to challenge the students with sight-reading and basic theory lessons.

- We are so concerned with playing and practicing the notes that we often lose sight of the overall intent of the composer. What feelings does this music evoke? How does that fit into our lives? Now, can we play that emotion?

Provide hands-on experiences.

- The music room should be loud. Make music...let the students experiment. Don't worry that the principal might walk by and wonder what's going on!

- Your band will be as good as the amount of playing they do together. Students join band to play, not hear an adult talk. Teach quickly, then *play, play,* and *play* again. Everyone will be happier with the result.

- As someone who is challenged every day by my students, one of my main aims is to try and get my students playing at the highest level that they can accomplish. In order to do this, I try to teach them music history and theory and then try to find a way to get them to play better using a technique that makes sense and works for them.

- Teach all aspects of music. Do not just sing with your students. Students need to play music. Students need to move to music. Students need to be able to sit *still* and listen to music.

Promote music for life.

- Approach music from a real-life standpoint. Most of our students will not become professional performers. So what skills and memories do you want your students to have from your music class ten, twenty, or thirty years from now?

- Make sure that kids know that there is a musical life beyond school. I try my best to encourage my students to think into secondary school and beyond about how they can use their musical knowledge.

- Create lifelong musicians. See your students in the future as adults. Teach to that future—creating a musical adult.

- Expose students to career options in music, as well as other careers with a musical connection. Let students know that there are a lot more career choices than simply music teaching and music performance; help them to explore not only areas like music publishing and business and music technology, but also nonmusical careers with potential musical connections, such as medicine (medical problems in musicians), engineering (music instrument design), architecture (designing music rehearsal and performance spaces), and wood/metalworking (music instrument building).

Provide listening opportunities.

- Taking students to live concerts is important so that students can see that music is a *living* art form—too often we only focus on dead composers. Students need a positive example for their growth.

Visit http://www.menc.org/industry/job/careers/careers.html for a glimpse of careers in music along with qualifications and salary ranges.

Check out a copy *Exploring Careers in Music,* 2nd ed. (Reston, VA: MENC, 2000) for information on a variety of musical careers.

- Make the school community aware of free and low-cost opportunities to hear music of different types and genres.

- Expose the children to music through field trips. Through these experiences, the children gain an understanding and appreciation for different types of music. For some students this may be the only opportunity to attend such an event; for others it opens a door to a brand-new experience.

- Train them to be audience members, as well as performers. Teach them also to demonstrate proper audience etiquette.

- Invite local musicians to share their talent. Music is something we share, and not all teachers have done all things in music. Realize your limitations and find people who have musical styles and experiences that you haven't had. Recording engineers, producers, opera singers, banjo players, musicians from other cultures...the list is endless and usually not very far from your classroom!

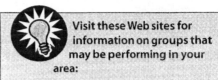

Visit these Web sites for information on groups that may be performing in your area:

- National Symphony Orchestra League, http://www.symphony.org/find/state/index.shtml#
- Opera America, http://www.operaamerica.org/perfdatabase.asp

Before taking your students to a concert, visit http://www.menc.org/guides/etiquette/etiquette_home.html for a guide to concert etiquette for students and parents.

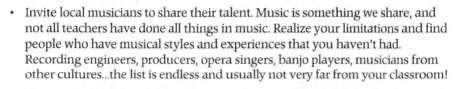

Being a choral director, I have had much success with listening with my students to fine (and sometimes not-so-fine) recordings. I encourage the students to evaluate the performance. They try to guess when it was written, giving facts to support their thoughts. I have found that students are tested so much they have become afraid to have a thought other than a vague, I hate this or like this. During these listening sessions, I am very careful to not judge their answers. They are becoming braver.

Whenever my orchestra gets in a rut, I drag out the CD player and put in an incredible CD of one of my favorite pieces. The kids are always amazed at the sound and inspired by the performance, and they like my reaction to the music. They always play with heart after they listen to professionals.

I have taken my vocal music students to see an opera each year for the past six years. This is an awesome experience. I now have students who have an appreciation for opera.

I took it as a personal triumph the day a senior purchased a recording of the Holst *Planets* after we played just a small portion of it. *All* the other CDs in his wallet were marked with the parental advisory (so you can tell what his "usual" taste was). He said he was surprised how he liked the *whole Planets* suite!

Use the best music.

- Study and select great literature. Even beginners can learn to appreciate good literature if you do your homework and pick music not just from the lesson book, but from the classics.

- Finding quality music for my ensembles is a continual search! I go to reading sessions, examine publishers' packets, listen to other groups, etc., etc., etc.

- As an elementary teacher, I am committed to using good music and teaching my children as much music history as they can consume. The results I have seen are astounding. I have parents telling me their children ask for Mozart CDs.

- Use the best music possible in order to establish the foundation for students' growth and understanding. Make the music relevant. Remember to give credit to new music as well as to that of the time-honored composers.

- I strongly feel my toughest job is choosing the right music. I spend the majority of my summers (1) deciding what I want the band to learn, (2) finding music that matches my learning objectives, (3) finding music the students will learn to enjoy, (4) finding music that satisfies me musically, (5) finding a variety of music that the audience will enjoy. None of the above is more important than the other. If the music does not fit all five criteria, I look for something else.

- Chose only music you *love*! Don't give in to the junk or things you think your students will like. If you don't love it, you'll hate it by the fiftieth rehearsal, and you'll never convince your students to like it or be able to promote excitement about it.

- When students enjoy a piece or musical work, they have fun playing it and will even practice it without being told to do so. At the same time, the selections should include appropriate learning materials and techniques that are found in a variety of musical periods and forms, including classical as well as "popular" tunes.

- Select music just above technical and musical abilities of students to make them reach new heights. It's important that students do not remain stagnant. What is difficult to them now will be easy later.

Visit the band, orchestra, and chorus literature lists at http://www.menc.org/channels.html for lists of suggested literature submitted my MENC members. Don't forget to add your own suggestions to the list!

Visit http://www.menc.org/information/allstate.htm for repertoire lists from all-state ensembles.

Offer a mix of difficulties to mixed-talent groups such as band. Have some selections that are challenging to the excellent students, average students, and least capable students. Each year work on a highly difficult selection—little by little if necessary. Try rotating first, second, third, and fourth parts so all students learn to play melody, harmony, etc., on some music.

Add new repertoire frequently. One of the best sources for band directors is the series *Teaching Music through Performance in Band* (Chicago: GIA Publications). There are books and CDs of excellent band music for the middle and high school level.

Try many types of music.

- Expose students to all styles of music—not what they are already listening to. And don't just focus on the "important" music. The world is full of musical styles that we as Americans miss out on. European music is just a small slice. Hook them with something, and then reel them into the other styles of music.

- Stay in the habit of varying the material (music genre). Brush up on the characteristics and composers of different music eras. You may lose interest from students if you generally only teach baroque music.

- Be eclectic in music selection. All styles of music have strengths and weaknesses. Students come from many backgrounds. I try to teach them to appreciate many different styles of music.

- At the elementary level, exposing the students to many different types of music is very important. If we don't grab them now, we might lose them.

- Use music from many areas of the world. Even in my rural school, there are students of various backgrounds and religions.

- Include the local music heritage. Everything is so geared toward multi-culturalism and teaching

During a Tri-M initiation, a student did a report on Philip Glass and minimalist music. I played my limited collection of minimalist CDs. Two of the members were amazed and captivated with the style (to the point of purchasing a Philip Glass CD for themselves)!

Last year I took a Japanese taiko dan drumming class from a local group. Wow! My new appreciation for the Japanese culture, their drummers, and the people who devote their lives to this art form has enriched my life. Then I managed to have the local taiko dan drummers come to both of my schools and give assembly performances. Then, with some old lummi sticks I've had for years, I was able to let the kids learn stick patterns and beat their aggressions out on carpet samples to the *Lion King* soundtrack music.

Growing up, I listened to the Beatles and developed an enjoyment of music from India. Years later, a friend sold me a sitar that I take to elementary school to show and play for the students. They are intrigued by the sound and have lots of questions.

I do music trivia during band. Using terms from music in their band folders, we have music trivia on a weekly basis. A question goes on the board on Wednesday, and they answer it on a slip of paper the following Wednesday and get a new question. I tape a candy reward onto the papers of those who get the question correct. Example questions are, What does *sfz* mean? What does *andante* mean? What are the three songs in this medley?

Music "Five a Day" is an idea I borrowed idea from a math teacher friend—five math problems a day are the first thing done when students enter the classroom. I have five music terms for students to identify. Sometimes I start with music reading and use rhythmic notation as well as pitch notation.

I created a "Rhythm Tree" made of posterboard and apples (die-cut). On each apple is a rhythm such as quarter note, quarter rest, or paired eighth. Because they are attached with Velcro, I can change the rhythm, and students can "compose" their own rhythms on the tree.

I do a composer of the week. Each week we listen to a different composer— anyone from Bach to Elton John. The students learn the country they were born in and when they lived as well as what they composed. This is sometimes related to events the students may be knowledgeable about (e.g., American Revolution). As they have gained proficiency in remembering composers, I have asked them to identify instruments that they hear. But be careful what you ask for. One week the composer was Richard Rodgers, and we were listening to the "March of the Siamese Children." I asked the students what instrument in this song made it sound like it was from an Asian country. In trying to elicit "gong" as an answer, after several students had been unsuccessful in coming up with the name, I described it. One student raised his hand immediately and excitedly. When I called on him, he said, "Thong." This was a third-grade class, and some of the students did know what *that* was.

I am switching to Kodály. My third graders, after two years of Kodály training, sight-read better than most of my high school choir!

I use a compilation of Orff, Kodály, Dalcroze, Pythagorus, Aristotle, and even a bit of Bob Marley along with Leonard Bernstein, Aaron Copland, and *Sesame Street*. I tell my students on all levels that these people changed the world through their musical ideas. On the elementary level, we dance our notes and jump up and down floor staffs, do phrases and lots of other Dalcrozian ideas along with rhythm counts based on Orff, melody hand signals based on Kodály, and anything else that will bring every multiple intelligence into play along with as many cultures as possible. We see, hear, and *do* Hawaiian drumming, African drumming, Celtic drumming, kodo drumming, mariachi music, classics, and a bit of *Stomp*—anything that piques their interest and imagination.

about everyone else's music that we sometimes forget to include the music that our own location/culture is known for.

- Use examples of contemporary music and materials to keep student interest at a high level. Review materials constantly to keep material fresh.

Teach musical skills.

- Ask, "What do they really need to know?" If they do not need to know how to write music using secondary dominants—don't do it. I have half an hour every week, and we barely have time to learn how to draw the notes, let alone do II chords.

- We need to teach fewer ideas in greater depth at all levels. I do not like smorgasbord approaches to elementary music education. We must stress the music of our own culture in depth and then branch out.

- Make a variety of music courses available to all students. Schools should offer a variety of music courses (band, chorus, ensemble, keyboard, general music, composition, theory, etc.) to students of *all* grade and ability levels. These courses should be offered for sufficient time periods as well (12–18 weeks minimum).

- Teach the elements of music. Understanding the elements is basic to developing an appreciation of music. Regular reinforcement is essential.

- Sound before sight! How simple it sounds! It goes back to the time of Lowell Mason and the foundations of American public music education, but this simple idea is so often ignored. *Teach music theory when it can no longer hurt (confuse!) the student.*

- Insist on students' learning to read music.

- Help students understand primary chords and cadences. Staying within the keys of C, G, and F, have students understand relationships between keys, the structure of chords, and their relationship to the key of the piece. Encourage experimentation and discuss weaknesses and strengths of chords used.

HALLE DINKLE   BY *TOM BATIUK*

- I use solfège with American folk songs, which are mini-classics. The use of the solfège hand signs keeps the students interested and able to understand the relationships between pitches and sing in tune.

- *Scales*!!!! Music is scales rearranged. I place a heavy emphasis on scale and arpeggio study in the classroom.

- Use daily rhythm drills to challenge rhythm reading and use of rhythm in the music that we perform.

- Include *skill building* in daily warm-ups, exercises, and the choice of music used in concerts and festivals. Include tone production, high and low range, tongue and finger facility, and a phrase a day to work on breathing and expression.

- Teach practice skills. Students need to understand that they are each responsible for the quality of the group, and they need to be taught practice techniques that make their time spent more effective. I have done lots of modeling in this area, and I also have kids tape their practice sessions for a grade and to show off what good "practicers" they are.

Try some sight-reading.

Teach the fundamentals of playing, including playing position, embouchure, breathing/breath support, tone, articulation styles... These are the building blocks to performing well. They cannot be stressed enough. Find subtle ways of reinforcing these in every rehearsal.

Try this articulation warm-up. At a tempo of 92–126 mm to the quarter note on a concert F, I start with two measures of half notes. I then go to two measures of quarters, eighths, eighth triplets, and finally sixteenths. The results of this type of daily exercise are clean attacks, even articulation, accurate counting of subdivisions, and better breath support.

All of my second-year band students have to be able to play all major scales (ascending and descending) as eighth notes at 92 mm to the quarter for one octave. This is to be done slurred and articulated. All of my third-year students have to do the same thing at 126–132 mm in various articulation patterns. This is gradually incorporated into the daily warm-up. All of my third-year students have to play all minor scales (all three forms ascending and descending) as eighth notes at 92 mm to the quarter. The accuracy of intonation of the students is greatly improved.

Try this dynamics control warm-up. On a concert F, have the students play a four-measure long tone starting at *ppp*, crescendo to *fff* at the first beat of the third measure, and diminuendo and hold the last quarter of the fourth at *ppp*.

- Sight-read daily. Sight-reading is only sight-reading one time. Using old abandoned music, new music, samples, traded music from other teachers, etc., will give you resources to constantly challenge students. Daily sight-reading will increase their ability to read music better the first time and lead to questions you can use to teach things they have forgotten or never learned.

- Sight-read consistently. This is not a once-a-month practice. It must happen as much as possible. Students cannot function as good musicians without knowing the language.

- In order to be good musicians, students should be exposed to sight-singing and have opportunities to listen to a piece of music and write out the melody more often in school.

Let students perform in small groups.

- Give students independent parts. Students should not just play unison exercises at the beginning level but must learn to maintain an independent musical part, rhythmically and melodically.

- Encourage solo work. Very few of my kids take any kind of private lessons; I see great improvement in both their abilities and their confidence when we work on solos for the solo and ensemble festival. I do *all* my solo instruction after school and usually have about fifty to sixty kids participating.

- Include chamber music during lessons. Students are amazing at following. I had a student in my top flute class. They all played exceptionally well, attended solo festivals, etc. It wasn't until the end of the third year when we were sight-reading trios that I discovered she did not know how to count at all. Even when sight-reading, she was so good at following, or remembering from hearing others play ahead of her, I never knew she couldn't count. Chamber music makes each student independent. It reinforces counting and playing what is written (versus what you hear going on around you), and it builds confidence. This has also worked incredibly well with percussionists who tend to fall into "boom-chick" patterns. Percussion ensemble teaches them to read the parts.

> I believe that teaching small-ensemble singing benefits the larger group. It introduces the students to more literature and develops independent musicianship. Our district festival choral results show that schools that enter many ensembles usually are the ones to consistently make Superiors at district and state evaluations.

- Use small groups to aid in bringing less-experienced players closer to the average playing level of the group.

- Use small groups to develop and encourage leadership and greater proficiency among the stronger players in the group.

Let students create.

- Encourage improvisation and composing. Help students realize that there is a time and place for freedom of expression and thought as well as absolutely accurate performance.

- I find that letting the students "help" me compose pieces makes them more eager to learn how to perform the piece well.

- Letting the students create and change music with help builds self-esteem and helps them to develop an open mind. This will also give them a different point of view toward music.

- In order to understand what they see and hear, students must compose and create their own music, even if it is very simple. For example, my chorus students are required to create a basic (or more difficult, if they are able) warm-up for rehearsal. They notate the rhythm and melody, and they lead the class at the beginning of rehearsal.

Provide performance opportunities.

- Music is a performance art—without sharing it, the study of music is self-serving. It is meant to be shared.

- Push for performance. Nothing improves student dedication like knowing that there is a concert scheduled on a specific date. Music is learned and skills are developed when there is a clear goal like a performance in the schedule.

- Students must be given every opportunity to perform. It is the fire that keeps kids interested and involved. Without performance, kids lose interest quickly.

- Provide lots of performance opportunities. Not only is it good for the students to perform in the community, it creates a great, positive image for the entire music program.

- My students enjoy sharing their musical creations. It is important to them to not only perform for parents, but also for peers and their other teachers. A "Well Done!" or "Good Job!" from the science or social studies teacher means a lot. However, performance must not be the sole motivating force behind the students' desire to make music.

- At the middle school level, students need something to work for. I like to find extra performing opportunities like pep rallies, outside concerts, and solo/ensemble contests as well as full-group contests. It sure beats just performing at two concerts a year.

- Provide information for students and their parents about performing opportunities other than their school organization and classroom lessons, such as the following: community or local youth bands or orchestras; regional and all-state band, orchestra, and chorus; summer camp opportunities; and so forth.

Prepare for all performances with care.

- Research calendar well in advance for open dates. Parents and community appreciate a concert on an opportune night...and students perform better for a known audience.

- Personally invite the principal and superintendent to address parents and students at concerts.

Every single one of my students is on stage at some point in the year. I do grade-level assemblies during the day so that I don't have to rely on parent transportation. Some parents (a very small number) do miss these assemblies, but the parents at my school *know* that I am first and foremost concerned with the opportunities of the children.

I do as many programs based on the music in the curriculum as possible. I teach in a low-income neighborhood with many bilingual children. The self-esteem they gain from programs is very important. The programs are also a way to educate the parents about the importance of music in education.

My students can experience music through a variety of means outside the music room. They perform in school musicals, my chorus performs throughout the community, and I take groups of students to a local nursing home each week for a music program. My students audition for and participate in all-state concerts, as well as a weekend chorus camp. These experiences help them to grow as musicians and boost their self-esteem.

Working with a group of folk musicians (former professionals who volunteer their efforts), we put on yearly shows that focus on links with social studies curriculum. Fourth grade is California history, fifth grade is early American songs, and sixth is an eclectic mix of jazz and drumming. Our fourth and fifth grade shows are very popular and only include authentic music. These shows are very important politically and help with the continuation of our program. The musicians are wonderful, and we music teachers play also and are featured on different songs that show our individual talents.

- Program only music that has the potential for success with your groups. No one likes to fail, and few, if any, adolescents are inspired by marginal performances.

- Don't put students up for a concert unless they are ready. It's not okay to say, "This will have to be good enough" or "It's okay, they're cute." Students don't want to be "cute," but they do want to be respected.

- Present varied programs. Perform music from various styles and time periods, some serious literature, some light, some pop. You need something for everyone at your concert. This keeps them coming back.

- Have the students help plan their programs. When students help with the choice of songs and actions, they perform much better because they are enjoying what they perform.

- Use choreography wherever possible. (John Jacobson is my hero.)

- In assembly programs, we try to give each child a chance to shine, whether it's in song, dance, drama, or art.

- Each child is able to participate in at least one program during the school year.

Programs are presented both afternoon and evening, so the community has ample opportunity to attend. This not only builds community support, but also gives the children a chance to develop their self-discipline, social and performing skills, and musicianship.

These publications by John Jacobson can help you add choreography to your concerts:
- *Dictionary of Dance: The Ultimate Guide for the Choral Director* (Milwaukee, WI: Hal Leonard, 1997)
- *Gotta Sing, Gotta Dance* (Milwaukee, WI: Hal Leonard, 1993)
- *John Jacobson's Riser Choreography* (Milwaukee, WI: Hal Leonard, 1993)

- Showing off student compositions using computers with MIDI equipment and a video projector at concerts results in a lot of "oohs and ahs" from the parents and administration. This does wonders in terms of gaining support for your music program.

Attend festivals.

- I thought my students would like singing for local organizations, but they preferred singing at festivals so they could hear other choirs.

- Being the only string program in the county, it is difficult for the students to have a benchmark for comparison. Taking them to a festival each year gives them (and me) the chance to receive comments from impartial adjudicators.

- Performing for adjudication keeps me on my toes, makes me listen to my ensembles more critically, and gives my kids a sense of accomplishment.

Teach life skills.

- Music is the medium, not the mission. The great mission is to help in the development of whole, integrated human beings who love themselves and their abilities and therefore bring more into the world, rather than take more from it. Our mission then is the whole picture, not just our part in it. We cannot become stuck in our own world, our own "place" in the school, but rather, we must function as a part of the whole for the whole child, for the whole community.

- Teach them about life. Students today are different from those of yesterday. They are into how this will affect their lives. We can teach them to present themselves in a positive manner, to work as a team and as an individual, to be flexible when faced with an unknown situation, to treat one another with respect (even if we disagree), to set a goal and achieve it, to have good work ethics. If we don't take the time to teach this to our students, who will?

- All of our students are consumers of the media. Better acquaintance with the possibilities (folk, classical, etc.) available will make them better consumers and more knowledgeable about what they do purchase. We need to educate them to make better choices on spending their money.

- Develop leadership through class procedures. I use small-ensemble opportunities to allow seventh graders to build leadership qualities.

- Focus on team building and teamwork. We start with a unit in the fall on team building and build from that. Students know that they can better themselves. This creates a supportive climate for learning.

- In all ways at all times we must encourage practice. To do this, we must also take time to teach our students skills in organization and time management.

Try an interdisciplinary unit.

- I regularly communicate with the grade-level teachers in my building to develop interdisciplinary units that are meaningful to my students. Incorporating other disciplines into my lessons gives the students a wider perspective on materials learned.

> When I talk to the sixth-grade social studies teacher and discover that students are working on Renaissance and medieval life, I can teach the unicorn songs and recorder pieces to the music class. I learn so much more about those periods when I cooperate with the history or social studies teachers.
>
> I recently taught history, science, math, literature, dance, music, visual art, and drama of the Renaissance period. The students were very receptive and motivated. Faculty also. I am now working on another idea involving clowns and the circus.

- Relating music to other subjects when appropriate not only helps students see connections, it also emphasizes the vast importance of music in our culture and encourages respect and support from classroom teachers for the music program.

- I try to create my own programs using a theme that is useful to other teachers so they will cooperate with the teaching and practices.

- Know the district benchmarks. I am familiar with the music benchmarks as well as those in the other disciplines as well. I incorporate language arts, math, and social studies into my lesson plans.

- Our kids will never appreciate music they are unfamiliar with without understanding where that music came from and why it was important to another generation or to another place.

CHAPTER 2

How Do I Teach All This?

O nce you have a handle on what you are going to teach, you have to decide how you are going to teach it. What steps must you go through to develop a great lesson plan? What do you need to do before class starts? What approaches are most effective at reaching the most students? How do you assess student learning? This chapter offers suggestions on developing lesson plans that will bring success to you and your students.

Set a goal.

- Keeping a specific goal for the year in mind helps me to focus on the big picture of what I want the students to learn.

- This is a journey. We are all headed toward a goal, and the journey is perhaps more important than the goal. The journey is a continuum, and goals are only intermittent marking signs.

- Set and communicate objectives, long and short term. This could range from the choice of music for a program to which measures or phrases will be covered during the second ten minutes of class.

- Create a yearly mission statement. Nothing produces success like knowing what I want to accomplish each year with my students. A mission statement allows me to set goals, time lines, and plans. It's a great tool and allows me to evaluate the success or failure of each class.

- Set goals with student involvement. The goals you set for your program are the blueprint for what you and the students will accomplish over the years. You must involve the students to get them to participate and to be enthusiastic about where you are going.

- Learn how to learn. How do you eat an elephant? One small bite at a time. Learning how to break up difficult tasks into manageable, success-oriented segments allows students to experience growth at different levels.

Have high standards.

- Maintain high musical standards. Avoid the temptation to pander to the lowest common denominator. Music is an art and as such requires dedication to the highest ideals.

- Set realistic and measurable musical goals. Setting goals that can be met and then meeting them ensures success at a basic level. Make sure that the students realize that they have met the goals and are therefore progressing. Success breeds more success, and as you continue to demonstrate this success, your achievements will continue to grow.

- Not only should the teacher help students meet high standards in performance and music learning, but the teacher should help students meet high standards in their personal behavior. Teachers should help students learn acceptable classroom behavior, appropriate audience behavior, successful practice strategies, etc. By maintaining high standards of behavior in addition to the high standards in music-specific activities, the teacher will help the students have success in all classes and throughout life.

- Dare to do the outrageous–think *big*! Students will live up to your expectations if you enable them through faith in their abilities!!!

- I expect excellence from my performing groups. That word can take on different connotations depending on the age of the group and the situation, but striving for excellence pushes each group to achieve at levels that they did not think possible at the beginning of the year.

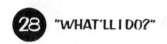 I like to let the students listen to a piece I'm fairly sure they will like that is a level above where they are presently playing. We'll listen to it several times throughout the year, and usually they will begin asking me if we can listen to it and if we have music for it. I "just happen" to have the music ready to pass out, and the kids are so excited about getting to play it that teaching the new techniques needed is fun and easy.

- Challenge the students with quality music. Students love a challenge that they can eventually achieve. At our school, we continually raise the bar, and the students never fail to meet our goals.

- By nature, kids will give only as much as they are expected to give. If we as teachers set the bar high, but not out of reach, kids naturally strive to reach that bar.

- Never underestimate the kids. The student who is abysmal in all other subjects may be just the one who grasps what you are saying and doing.

- I have yet to find the point where they refuse to be pushed. Sometimes they need incentives (a sticker if you can play your chromatic scale, a sparkly sticker if you can play it memorized), but they are willing to be pushed as far as they

> Quality is expected. When the children sing and are not being conscious of matching pitches, I challenge them to address it. It seems that children are not conscious of the importance of matching pitches—or else the children I am seeing have no one else telling them—or modeling for them—the way we sing in tune.

can go. Sometimes with a little push, they exceed my expectations and go farther than I thought they could have!

- Challenge your students, but do not frustrate them.

- Be a role model! If you place high expectations on yourself and live up to them,

it will be more reasonable to place high expectations on the students, and the success rate will be raised.

Share your goals with students.

- When students know what is expected, they rise to meet and fulfill those expectations.

- Students must know what is on the agenda and how to achieve it.

- Make clear your expectations. If you share your expectations for behavior, practicing, maintenance of the instrument, etc., there will be no question as to where you stand if a question arises.

- I like to present the objective as a challenge—students love to realize they *can* do it!

- Put objectives on the board for students to see.

- Teaching is more effective when students understand the daily and long-term goals. They respond to the teacher who demonstrates exactly how this lesson (or subject) will affect their daily lives now and in the future. It is also wise to point out to students later in the year: "Remember when we learned (fill in the blank)? That was preparing you for this moment."

Have a long-term plan.

- Plan and prepare meticulously. I plan my year, week by week and lesson by lesson, before the year starts.

- Plan well in advance. Being one step ahead of the students (or parents, administrators, etc.) means that you really have to be looking far in advance all the time. Knowing how many classes are left in the year/semester to accomplish what you want to can make the difference between actually getting it done and running out of time in the middle of a project.

- Organization and long-range planning are essential for successful teaching and learning to take place. Students will not take music study seriously when it is apparent that the teacher is confused and unprepared. This lack of respect for music class also leads to lack of discipline. When students are actively involved in making music, because the teacher uses well-thought-out pedagogical techniques, it is much easier to keep students in line.

- Lesson plans aren't something to be done on Sunday night before the next school day. I have an overall plan for kindergarten through third grade and am working on overall plans for fourth through sixth grade. I leave myself some flexibility in my week-to-week planning, but I try to stick to my yearly plans to keep myself on track.

- Long-term goals and plans, as well as daily lesson plans, are important in creating and sustaining a good school music program.

Don't wing it!

- Be prepared. Class always goes much better when you know what you are doing and what comes next, and when you have your materials ready and at hand.

- "If you fail to plan, you plan to fail." The days that I think winging it will be easier than taking the time to plan a lesson are typically a semidisaster with a minimum of progress made toward any short- or long-term goal.

- I teach with a plan. I'm organized and know where I want to go and how to get there. Without a plan, discipline becomes a problem.

- A lot of the time, I feel I could go to any of my classes and just wing it. This may be a tempting way to get through the day, but it does not benefit the students. Plan more than you think you can do in one class time, and you can accomplish a lot more.

> I develop a plan for each rehearsal. I limit my time on each objective (e.g., students will perform measures 12–20 with rhythmic accuracy). This keeps me focused on the goals for the rehearsal and also keeps me from spending too much time on any one piece. I list the plan on the board in front of the choir. The visual reference helps them keep track of their goals and how to utilize their time best during the rehearsal.

- I plan each step of the lesson, aimed always at my objective, with clear directions so the children can achieve the learning goal.

- Plan your rehearsal and stick to the plan. A structured rehearsal means less wasted time. Posting what will be rehearsed reduces transition time.

- Plan *everything*–especially for unanticipated occurrences. There should be nothing that isn't anticipated!

- The best way to be in control is to be prepared. I feel it is important to stay more than one step ahead of the student. I must be a true professional and spend a sufficient amount of time on the subject matter.

- When my students enter the room, I am ready to teach and all materials are prepared. We have set routines, and I have set expectations. I expect them to be ready to learn. I keep lots of notes to help me stay on top of their needs and progress.

- Be prepared for rehearsals. It is, after all, the most important way we have of affecting our students. Don't blow it by wasting your time together.

- Be ready to go when the kids come in. Have your lessons planned out and ready to go from one item to the next without hesitation. This also means be on time—don't be late.

- Structure class activities. Provide students with a specific structure for learning new information and skills. For example, when composing a song, practicing an instrument, or writing a paper, provide the students with a detailed process for completing the task. Using study guides, where appropriate, enables students to learn basic information outside of class so that class time may be devoted to clarifying concepts and the practical application of material.

- Have a daily schedule, but vary it sometimes. Students, especially younger ones, need structure in their classes and rehearsals, but don't let it stagnate. They will let you know when it's time for a change, if you listen.

Know your stuff.

- I am a better teacher if I am musically well prepared for rehearsal. That means that I need to know my music well. Score study allows me to know the music intimately and have an aural image of the what the music communicates. Having a clear image of the music also allows me to both intentionally and unintentionally use the correct conducting gesture to show the shape of the music.

- I do extensive research in order to have a broad understanding of the musical concepts, events, etc., that I teach. I make sure that I understand the history surrounding holidays or special days. I make sure that I know the biographies of the composers I teach about—especially their growing-up years, so that students can better relate to them. I make it my business to understand many things when I teach my music class.

- Thoroughly learn a song before introducing it to the students. Being a new choir director, I find it somewhat difficult to learn a song completely before introducing it to the students. It means a lot of extra time, but it just has to be done!

- Do your homework on the music before presenting it. Questions about phrasing and dynamics should be answered from the beginning of rehearsals.

- Music students are a whole lot more perceptive than we give them credit for being. They can tell when you are feeding them a line of misinformation. If you don't know something *for sure*, ask the student to come with you and look up the information in question. They will appreciate it much more.

- Be able to answer questions on what you are teaching. If you are always saying, "I'll have to look that up," kids will begin to think you do not know what you are doing.

Develop a sequential curriculum.

- Begin with what students know, and build on that basic knowledge with sequential instruction.

- Create a strong, connected curriculum. Without a curriculum that builds on itself from year to year, the students will either relearn old material or not learn important skills, and therefore not be able to move forward.

- Ensure that music is taught in a complete sequential K–12 program. Even in districts with more than one school, there must be a sequential and standardized curriculum to be used when teaching music. High school teachers must be involved in the lower grades and teachers in lower grades should remain involved in aspects of the upper school programs.

- Adhere to the National Standards. The National Standards for Music Education are posted in my classroom and are referred to on a daily basis. Students are not only learning and gaining musical knowledge and skills, but they know what and why they are learning.

- I can't imagine trying to learn anything that is sequential without first having been taught the prior building blocks that will enable my success!

- Bloom's Taxonomy *must* be a driving force in designing any systematic approach to band instrument and music-reading knowledge and skill building.

 Visit the MENC Web site (http://www.menc.org/publication/ books/standards.htm) for more on the National Standards for Music Education and links to information on state standards.

Visit http://www.teachervision.fen.com/lesson-plans/lesson-2171.html for a brief overview of Bloom's Taxonomy of Educational Objectives, or just type "Bloom's Taxonomy" into an online search engine. For details, see Benjamin Bloom's *Taxonomy of Educational Objectives: The Classification of Educational Goals: Handbook I, Cognitive Domain* (New York: Longmans, Green, 1956).

Knowing what has to be known, understood, internalized, and demonstrable before each new developmental step is taken greatly increases the chances for success over the long run.

Try something new.

- Constantly create new lessons to present the same information. Even when a lesson plan works well, doing the same lessons year after year makes me stale. So even when I repeat a lesson, I try to do something different with it.

- Try to teach a new topic each year. While teaching elementary general music, I realized I had never taught the twelve-bar blues. One year, I decided to research the blues and teach it to my class. I had to research because the superficial understanding I had wouldn't have been sufficient to answer the myriad questions my students would pose. Each year I found another topic I had never shared.

- Develop new lesson plans each year. Since the same students pass through the music class each year, I try to develop new plans to keep my motivation strong and keep the students guessing as to what new and wonderful things they will do in music class.

- Kids are easily bored, so be sure to have lots of tricks in your bag to vary classroom method. Kids will naturally focus when they are challenged with something new. Consistent classroom management is important, but vary the methods within the consistency.

- I must constantly work to find new ways to bring instruction that is tailored to each group of students.

Use a variety of approaches.

- Explain concepts several different ways. Each child processes information differently. Some children are visual, some really are more aural, and some learn better by experience.

- Teach concepts in several different ways. For example, teach rhythm through standard counting and through using simple words like "Mississippi" for four sixteenth notes and "motorbike" for two sixteenths and an eighth.

- Offer new musical experiences. Students should have experiences in middle school that are different from those in elementary school (e.g., keyboards vs. recorders and Orff).

- Ten- and eleven-year-olds are constantly changing. What fascinates them this week is old hat next week. Incorporating mariachi, world music, rote learning, peer-teaching, games, movement, and different motivation ideas for practicing are some of the methods I utilize.

- Differentiate instruction. Not every kid will be able to experience success with every activity. If we as music teachers can design lessons including enough variation, we can teach and reach more kids.

- Every class and every student is unique. It helps to always be aware of how a class or individual responds and reshape the lesson presentation to accommodate this.

- Make the presentation of techniques in as few words as possible. If it doesn't work, then you have to try again with different phrasing. Sometimes your students will surprise you and get it right the first time. You have now saved time and can move on.

- Welcome new ways of learning. I like for my students to make up new ways to teach a concept—a person learns more by teaching than by being a passive learner.

- Use visuals. I use visuals to demonstrate all aspects of music to my classes. They remember much longer with a picture or graphic to accompany the concept.

> Try singing to match pitch for good intonation. If students can sing a pitch, they will play it correctly. I have tried experimenting with beginning bands, not even telling them what it was for. As long as the instrument is close enough, they will play more in tune after singing a note in tune. It doesn't solve all the problems, but it's a great way to begin.
>
> I had some kids in the marching band who could play beautifully and in tempo; however, they could not march in time. So I brought a boom box to the practice field, and instead of marching basic block, we did simple moves to the time of the popular music. ("Tainted Love" was their favorite.) The kids could move in time with that music, and we used it to get them to march in time as well.
>
> I found it more musical to place the stronger students throughout the section, not necessarily in chair order all of the time. This makes for better balance and a more musical end product. It also takes some education to have the students understand this approach.

Keep students active and interested.

- For students to learn, they have to actively be participating in the process. It is highly important to limit "teacher talk" and set-up time, as well as keeping ahead of any off-task behaviors.

- Pace rehearsals and classes well. Students are used to TV and videos and expect changes constantly. Pace your lessons and rehearsals similarly, and you will keep them on task and involved. It's also more fun!

- Let students choose the activity and material sometimes.

- Keep students actively involved. Everybody gets to try a little bit of everything. There is not a lot of waiting for turns in my classroom.

- Look at the lessons from a child's point of view. Don't sit or stand too long; vary the posture and type of activity the students will engage in throughout a lesson.

- Use variety in quickly paced plans. Use games and especially attractive activities as much as possible. Work consistently in small segments on intense skills such as sight-reading.

- Exploration is essential to the young child. Give children ample time to explore the sounds they can make. They should be taught to perceive and to describe sounds. Guide the children to respond appropriately to sounds all around them.

- Music and movement go hand in hand. Research shows that children are kinesthetic learners. They naturally move to music as well as hear it. Let them express themselves on their own terms initially. Help them, at first, by supplying vocabulary. Stress steady beat.

- Give practice opportunities. Sometimes I need to use an entire period just to let them practice concepts or patterns previously introduced. My classes are only thirty minutes long, so reviewing and practicing on subsequent days is essential for solid learning. It also leads nicely into improvisation.

- In my sixth- and seventh-grade classes, I try to develop a love for singing. We

I begin each class with a welcome song. I have a different welcome song for each grade level. At the end of first grade, I teach the second-grade song and begin solfège echos so that next year they will have prior knowledge.

Our students enjoy "center time" as a six-week reward for good behavior. Centers include books on music, theory, puzzle and coloring sheets on music, toy instruments to play (saving the "real" instruments for music class), "dress up" center for dramatic flair, games such as music dominos, music dart board, music twister, and a "dance" center that features a dance video. Kids love it!

Although many pedagogical techniques are effective, it is up to the teacher to provide balance between the mechanics of reading and writing music and the aesthetic qualities that make music art. A meaningful music-learning experience provides both. Many children I teach whose previous music teachers were Kodály-oriented read and write music beautifully but have no sense of nuance, phrasing, or improvisation. Children whose previous teachers were Orff-oriented usually can play ostinatos on Orff instruments as they sing a song and improvise appropriate sounds and motions for story dramatization but can't read or write music worth a hill of beans.

start our classes every day by singing familiar songs to warm up and learn new songs to add to our repertoire.

- Use authentic activities. Incorporating the "real-life" (authentic) use of material in the classroom is exciting and motivating in any subject area. As soon as possible, enable students to apply course information in ways that model real-life applications.

- Relate musical topics to everyday activities. When I am explaining a concept, I try to use as many things as possible that the students can relate to. For example: breathing. You have to play a four-measure phrase. You need to get enough air for four measures. You are a center fielder in baseball and have to throw the ball from the wall to home plate. You need to wind up and put enough energy into the throw so it can reach home plate.

Review and reflect.

- Keep reviewing concepts over and over...Sometimes the sheer repetition of a concept is what children grasp and successfully process.

- Review material each day. Due to limitations in grading for my subject area, I have found that a daily review of material covered in the previous few lessons genuinely aids the learning process.

- The best ideas are useless unless they are coordinated with pre- and post-activities that reinforce them.

- Take time to reflect with the students. After participating in the music making, don't forget to stop and reflect with the students about how the music was made, how it sounded, and what its components were.

Use the right materials.

- Use age-appropriate materials. It is important to offer students experiences that are appropriate for their age.

- Use the right equipment. If students are using poor equipment, they will get a bad sound.

- I have greatly enhanced the lessons I teach through the use of programs like PowerPoint, Front Page, and Sibelius. The students have also used these programs in class. Having music Web pages helps me to keep students and parents informed as well.

- Technology is used heavily in my classroom. Computers, digital electronic keyboard, and the MIE (Music in Education) system turn theory into actual practice and performance of music–*real learning*!

To learn more about Yamaha's Music in Education (MIE) program, visit http://www.musicineducation.com.

For more on how to use technology in your classroom, visit the MENC Technology Network at http://www.menc.org/networks/technology/technology.html or see the following MENC publications:
- *Strategies for Teaching: Technology* (2002), compiled and edited by Sam Reese, Kimberly McCord, and Kimberly Walls.
- *Spotlight on Technology* (2003), a collection of articles from state MEA journals.

Be flexible.

- Always look for new ways of teaching. This way you don't get stuck in your ways and miss out on something. Also, this gets you excited about teaching a fresh way and poses challenges for you to teach the subject matter most effectively.

- Be able to alter course or abandon ineffective practices.

- Think fast on your feet. I have to be very aware of my students and monitor how they feel–if they are getting frustrated–if something is too easy–if they are bored. Then, I must adjust what I am doing to keep them interested and learning.

- Flexibility is key. Think on your feet. Expect the unexpected. Stay mellow and keep your head when others are losing theirs...because they will!

- The unexpected loves to happen. Better to be able to change gears fast than mourn for the loss of a "perfect" lesson plan.

- Be flexible in your lessons. Sometimes students have problems and can't exactly absorb the lesson of the day. Know when to modify your plan for the day and still teach something to someone.

- It is important to keep the material fresh so students will find the music interesting and remain involved in the program. It is also important to be willing to modify the music to the students' proficiency levels and to revise the program according to the students' needs.

Change an activity or lesson that doesn't work well the first time. Adapt lessons to fit your needs or to simplify for your students. For example, while we were working on the World's Largest Concert, the Orff lesson for "Silver Moon Boat" was proving too difficult for my third graders. I simplified it and added scarves on the phrases, which we needed to work on anyway. We also added finger cymbals, and it worked much better.

- It doesn't matter how well I have thought out my lesson plans; classes respond in different ways, and I need to be able to react appropriately. If more examples are needed, I need to be able to come up with them. If students react negatively toward something, I need to be able to turn it around into something positive.

- Go with the students' interests and ways of learning. If you know they learn best a certain way, do your best to adapt your teaching style to fit the students. It should be the students' best interests that a teacher has at heart!

- You constantly need to create new teaching techniques in the classroom. Also, occasionally a teachable moment appears and you have to take it even though it wasn't in the day's plan. Thinking on your feet is essential.

- Even though you may have your lesson well planned, we all know that the best-laid plans often go astray. Be flexible and willing to spend time showing the students how a piano works when they have questions after a student has shared a piano solo. They will remember this information because they have the interest at that time.

Assess student learning.

- Authentic assessment ensures that all students are being assessed against a common standard.

- Assessment is something I do on a daily basis, as I am sure many teachers do. It might not be a formal written assessment; however, if you do not assess what the students are doing in a particular class, you won't know what should be done in the next music class.

- There are many ways to test students' ability and move them forward. Most of the time, the students are not aware that I am listening for their pitch matching, rhythm echoing, etc. By evaluating the class members, I can tailor lessons to improve the weakest areas (e.g., spend more time on pitch matching if that is the weakest area).

- Constant assessment (formal and informal) ensures that what has been taught

HALLE DINKLE   BY TOM BATIUK

is being learned. If the knowledge or skills have not been acquired, we need to find another way to present them. All too often we assume that simply because we taught it, they have learned it. Constant informal questioning, as well as formal assessment, will provide us with the information we need in order to ensure the success of our students.

> In order to know whether the children actually learn what is taught, it is imperative to objectively test them individually at regular intervals. Beyond the primary level, most students will not put forth the effort to learn difficult skills that will not be formally evaluated. It's easier to follow along with someone else's sight-singing or rhythm reading than to learn how to do it yourself. One year I assumed that my second graders were doing an outstanding job sight-singing *sol–mi–la* patterns. When I tested them, all but four failed abysmally. I did a lot of reteaching, making sure that the few who understood did not mask others' weaknesses.

- Students need continuous feedback on their performance and progress.

- Keep track of your students' progress in writing. You should know how all of your students stand in their individual progress—keep this written down because we all see quite a few students during the day. This way you also have some written information when it comes to grading time or parent-teacher conferences.

- Take the time to document students' progress and show the students the results.

Students learn best by knowing what is expected and by seeing the results of the grading process. They will know how to continue to grow.

- Assess individual progress. Even quick and dirty measurements are better than relying on your memory. Come up with a system to measure what is important about the music program and then stick with that system. Refuse to allow a district to reduce your report card to an effort-only grade.

- Prioritize and focus criticism to a few salient points. Too much information at one time overwhelms and discourages.

- Test individually using a tape recorder. Assigning individual grades in an ensemble of thirty or forty can be difficult! I've found that individual testing with a tape recorder really makes kids work harder and gives me something solid on which to base grades.

- Use various types of assessments. Some assessments are pencil and paper, but others are listening or playing.

- Use portfolios. Students keep assignments, tests, handouts, notes, etc., in a portfolio, and they turn it in at various times during the semester. The teacher can use these portfolios to determine progress.

- Let students self-evaluate. It's amazing how perceptive students are when they help evaluate and listen for certain criteria in their peers' performances.
- Students should know what success means in the context of a given assessment. If you have a vocal rubric, students should know what excellence looks like. Self-evaluation is a great tool. As students learn to use the assessment, provided it's a quality measure, they also learn much more about the skills and content that constitute excellent or expert work.

Evaluate yourself.

- I frequently reflect on rehearsals and lessons and decide what went right and what didn't. Did the band improve that day, and why or why not? What state standards did I fulfill? Did I reach my goals for the rehearsal? I am constantly examining my teaching and trying to improve and streamline rehearsals.

- You must practice listening: hearing what your students are *really* saying about the material, the instruction, the goals. Since the next step you take is based upon what is needed by students, hearing what they have to say and being able to filter the wealth of material from the chaff of the nonsense that is said is very important.

- If something didn't work or wasn't good, find out why! Be extremely self-critical. If you're your toughest critic, everyone else is easy!

- I believe in evaluating myself as a teacher, both in writing and mentally during my teaching. I believe the students should be given the opportunity to evaluate the lessons and the teacher in a safe, nonthreatening manner.

- Videotape a rehearsal and evaluate your teaching style and practices.

- I periodically review and evaluate my teaching style and whether I am practicing clear and proper conducting techniques. It's easy to become more verbal while conducting ("Drummers, you're *too loud*") rather than letting the baton and the left hand communicate effectively. I am considering videotaping some of my classes, but so far haven't gotten up the nerve to face what I actually do that has room for effective improvement.

- Having people observe me helps me to see myself through the eyes of others, so that I can continue to do some things and make improvements in others.

2

"I Will Survive"

Classroom Management

"Did you hear what I think I said?" Teachers often ask this question, or something like it, of students who are not doing what is expected of them. Sometimes these teachers are in the midst of a poor learning environment with too many disruptions caused by a lack of organizational planning and provisioning for each class. The result? Confusion!

"My kids perform poorly, and I know that I am telling them the correct musical information." Oh, how many times have teachers said this? What is the cause? Teachers may say something like, "These kids just don't pay attention" or "It has to be this community!" In reality, the cause is often the teacher's lack of organizational skills and not providing a focus for each and every class. When this happens, discipline problems become apparent, and learning does not take place. Do the students understand the expectations of the teacher in all facets of the classroom, including behavioral expectations and musical expectations? Is the teacher positive to all students?

Too often, teachers overlook the obvious when dealing with the lack of a good learning environment in the classroom or rehearsal room. In this section, you will read several suggestions for successful classroom management and organizational ideas to help even the experienced teacher in the music classroom. You may already be doing many of the things described in this section. But, if one or two ideas spark a new thought, there will be growth in this all-important area of teaching.

Moe Turrentine
State Manager, Virginia Music Educators
   Association
Retired Coordinator of Fine Arts,
   Fairfax County, Virginia

CHAPTER 3

How Can I Get the Students to Behave?

anaging classroom activities is perhaps the greatest challenge many teachers face. The energy that students bring to music class can mean a productive and exciting rehearsal, but it can also mean an uphill struggle to get the musical goals accomplished. This chapter delves into teachers' ideas for making sure that student behavior is appropriate for the tasks at hand.

Make classroom management a priority.

- No question, discipline in the classroom will increase the amount of learning that can happen in the class period.

- If the discipline structure is in place in the music classroom, it makes even challenging tasks easier to teach and easier for the kids to grasp.

- When the classroom is managed in an effective, positive manner, students are more able to focus on the activities at hand. They are much less frustrated, and their overall performance is greatly improved.

- Kids want discipline! Kids need discipline!

- I consider myself the barometer of the classroom. I set the tone and the pace. If I don't do that, the kids are at sixes and sevens and can't learn.

> I took over a middle school choir classroom during the spring semester of this past school year; the previous teacher had no classroom management skills, and it showed in both the way the students acted and in how they sang. The first thing I did was to establish discipline and order. I felt that without that, there was no chance for the students to learn to sing. Once discipline was learned, the students began to make great progress in their singing abilities.

Learn more about the Boystown method at http://www.girlsandboystown.org/pros/training/education/ed_model.asp

Visit http://www.tribes.com to learn about Tribes Learning Communities.

Information about ITI (Integrated Thematic Instruction) is available at http://www.kovalik.com

Harry K. Wong and Rosemary Wong's *The First Days of School: How to Be an Effective Teacher* (Mountainview, CA: Harry K. Wong Publications, 1998) offers practical help on managing a classroom.

Classroom Management in General, Choral, and Instrumental Music Programs (Reston, VA: MENC, 2001) by Marvelene C. Moore, with Angela L. Batey and David M. Royce, offers classroom management suggestions specifically geared toward music teachers.

- Classroom management is extremely important. First of all, it endears you to the administration; second, you cannot reach the group's goals if you are constantly distracted by discipline problems; and thirdly, in today's society children need discipline and structure.

- I have been through TRIBES and ITI model training. Both have enriched my teaching and classroom management. TRIBES training is especially useful in reducing problem behaviors during class.

- My school uses the Boystown method, and it has been great for the students who want to learn and the teachers. I suppose many consistent systems could be applied schoolwide for similar results, but we train them for success this way. The rest of teaching is easier this way!!!

Maintain an orderly environment.

- If you can't keep control of the class, the best lesson plan in the world won't teach them anything.

- A rehearsal that is not well disciplined will waste time and effectiveness.

- If you don't have control of your classroom, you can't teach and the students can't learn.

- Learning cannot take place in an undisciplined environment. Students have pride and respect in their organization when it is self-disciplined.

- If they're not listening, they're most

I found it much more productive to warm up together; therefore, *no* blowing before, or after, class.

Get class started on time. My band students have ninety seconds at the beginning of class to unpack, check the board for the day's work, have music and books ready, and be at concert rest. If they're not ready within the allotted time, a notation is made in the grade book, and points are subtracted from the daily grade at the end of the grading period.

often not learning. Creating an environment of quiet attentive respect in the rehearsal (which thankfully spills over into all other segments of the education process) allows students to recognize the importance of consistent focus from themselves, as well as from their choral colleagues.

> I am a stickler for how kids sit in my elementary music room. Bottoms on the floor at all times. Sometimes I feel like I'm teaching sitting rather than music, but if the kids lack the self-discipline to sit in the best way for learning, they won't learn my topic for the day, anyway.

- Learning cannot take place in chaos. The more I become aware of learning disabilities and the increasing number of students who are identified with learning disabilities, the more I am convinced that distractions hinder many children from learning.

Teach discipline.

- Teaching skills of discipline (how to listen, social skills, communication, etc.) builds a foundation for all learning and makes time management practical.

- Students are taught to take responsibility for the equipment and the environment in my classroom. A class's productivity depends on behavioral as well as equipment management.

- I believe that a music program is an excellent medium for teaching discipline, self-respect, and responsibility. These days, many parents do not believe that they are responsible for their child's actions, behavior, or moral values. While I believe these areas of personal discipline should be primarily taught at home, I am finding that teachers are having to do more for these students in regards to discipline.

- Discipline and providing structure for students is so much more crucial now than it was even ten to fifteen years ago when I was a student. Regrettably, for too many of our students, we provide in our music classrooms the only boundaries/social structures/family structures they will see in their lives. So this aspect of what we do, while it should not overshadow the quality music education we seek to deliver, is taking on more and more significance in our profession, and we cannot over-emphasize this practice of our profession.

> I start the year with five very basic rules and then make sure all students learn them by having them said as a round, with movement, and anything else we can think of to cement them. I have two students each month help me monitor behavior with rewards for classes that consistently get terrific marks for cooperation.

Make your expectations clear.

- Be consistent and clear. Establish clear classroom rules and procedures that are always the

HALLE DINKLE BY TOM BATIUK

same and review them frequently, especially at the beginning of the year and when new students join the class. Changing these things very often is very confusing and frustrating for some students.

- Before beginning any musical concepts at the beginning of the year, I focus on discipline first. It saves a lot of headaches later.

- A music department handbook outlines expectations and consequences from the first day of school.

- Set a standard and stick to it, but make sure that your students understand what the standard is. Without any standards, how do you judge which student gets punished for certain behaviors? You will get a lot of "But you let Johnny say that" or "That's not fair, how come she gets to sit wherever she wants and I have to sit here?"

- You must set clear behavioral boundaries. Students must know exactly what behavior is encouraged, tolerated, and not tolerated. You must be consistent. You can be strict, but you must be fair.

- If the students know what they can and cannot do, they will not waste the time to do it; therefore, participation goes up.

- By making a clear statement of what is to be accomplished during each rehearsal *and* adhering to strict discipline principles, the director will find more time to accomplish goals while allowing for fun/free activities for the students as a reward.

I made up a "piano driver's" license, a music helper's license, and a guitar-carrying license. I'm on a cart, so at the beginning of each period, while I take attendance, I hand out the licenses to two or three students who are next in line to help. All the students understand that they can "lose" their license if they do something inappropriate. Very rarely do I have to take a license away from a student.

Be consistent.

- Have fair rules and be consistent in enforcing them. My students know the rules and understand why they are important in choir, and because I enforce them consistently, without bias, they work.

- Consistency is important in maintaining a functional classroom. Inconsistency leads to questioning of authority, which can interrupt the ability to be fair. Equal consequences for *all,* even your best student.

- Have a firm but fair discipline policy. Rules are made and discussed in class meetings, and we implement a lot of "love and logic" techniques.

- It is impossible to have good discipline and management in the classroom if you're not consistent and fair when dealing with issues that come up in the classroom. I think that failure to be consistent and fair will hurt the classroom environment and respect for the teacher faster than anything.

- My students say that an educator's efforts to establish and consistently enforce policies concerning class attendance, assignment due dates, and grading policy increase student self-discipline. These policies result in satisfactory performance from the majority of students and often prevent potentially lackadaisical students from doing poorly.

> I greet the class by singing a short "Hello" melody, and students respond by singing a taught response while they are passing out materials, etc. I end the classes the same way. This saves a lot of unnecessary noise and movement at the start and finish of class.

Establish procedures.

- I have a well-established program of rules, consequences, and rewards, and the students respond very well to it.

- Kids have to know what to expect in a classroom. Teachers must be very careful not to give mixed signals, which might confuse consistency. Kids will be creative and will perform their best in an environment that is stable and predictable.

> Use procedures for transitions. Our students practice procedures for transition times, such as putting away books, lining up to leave class, answering questions. These procedures are practiced on a daily basis so students are familiar with expectations in the music class.

- Begin on time with a set warm-up or ritual. Kids need clues to start the class without being yelled at.

- Much time and confusion can be saved for both teachers and students by following some basic standard procedures. Everyone knows what to expect.

- Have warm-up activities ready for kids when they walk in the door. Don't let a bell start your class; have the kids start it.

Keep kids on task.

- I find that when my lessons are thought out and prepared well, I have no discipline problems...at all!

- The best instructional strategies in the world are lost if students aren't paying attention.

- It is very important to keep students on task when I only see them for thirty-five minutes at a time.

- If I have techniques that motivate my students and keep their attention, then my teaching is already easier.

- Keep students on their toes. Don't become predictable. If the students don't know what to expect, they will pay closer attention.

- For my chorus class, I must limit the amount of down time and "talk" time on my part. If I don't keep the kids singing, they immediately start visiting with each other.

- Keep the children *actively* involved. In the very short time that we have with the children, they need to be actively engaged in playing their instrument. If the teacher spends too much time talking or explaining or demonstrating, there will be discipline problems, and the students will tune out the explanations. Few words, lots of playing, lots of interaction one-on-one and through the group.

Stay positive.

- Ignore as much negative behavior as possible. Music needs to be enjoyable. If students exhibit negative behavior, but it does not seem to affect the climate of the classroom or distract from the learning of others, just go on and enjoy the lesson. The other students deserve your attention. Also, many times students will change their mood or attitude if left alone just for a bit.

- In my classroom, I allow the students to talk (a little), but they know when they have gone too far.

- There are few behavior problems in a classroom where positive attention and recognition are given to students who demonstrate effort and good citizenship.

One of the things I do to keep students on task is called "Note-Worthy Behavior." I make a bulletin board display titled "Note-Worthy Behavior." On it I have staves marked with each home room's grade code. Each class that they behave, I allow a student to put a note on the staff. (Velcro works well.) Once they get the seven letters of the musical alphabet on their staff, the class gets to play a music game. On the other hand, if a class is not behaving well, they either do not get a note or they lose a note. A class may earn more than one note per class. Some classes earn a game each class period.

A teacher's compassion toward students goes a long way in helping to prevent problems and not having to wait to focus on the cure to one.

- Discipline should be strict but not overpowering. Students in music learn creativity, but they also need to learn through self-discipline. Learn to teach music with enjoyment and excitement not only for students but also for yourself.

- If a teacher uses harsh words to discipline a student, the student will in turn use those same words toward another student or back at the teacher.

> Once I got my own phone in my band room, the first time a discipline problem arose, I had the student go to the phone and contact the parent, where in front of the entire class, our conversation could be heard. Bottom line, I didn't have any discipline problems after this first incident.

> My eighth-grade chorus will socialize in the back of the room forever if allowed. (They're not technically tardy because they are in the room.) Because they are a large group, they pretend to be totally oblivious to start-up activities. However, they move really fast when I have the seating chart section leaders start giving "late minuses" to take away earned points.

- Stay calm (or at least act that way). I teach middle school—a sea of raging hormonal emotions! In discipline and classroom management, calmness and rationality are a must. Save your emotional outbursts for displaying your passion to students regarding the music, the music making, and communicating to your audience.

- Many of my students have difficult home and school lives and are looking for a safe place. My class rules make it clear that my class will be a safe and caring learning environment where nobody will be allowed to make fun of or tear down another person.

Follow through with consequences.

- Don't let anyone get away with anything. As Barney Fife would say... "Nip it in the bud." Don't back down once a decision has been made.

- Know your school's discipline protocol and take full advantage of it. They need to know you mean business!

- Know what classroom teachers use for discipline.

- For discipline, parent contact is important. If you have a problem that is beyond the control of normal discipline procedures, one call to the parents is usually all it takes.

CHAPTER 4

How Can I Stay Organized?

No doubt about it, music teaching is a tough job, one with lots of details that the music teacher must handle. Staying organized and managing your time effectively is an ongoing battle—but it's one worth fighting. Because music teachers have so many responsibilities, they have a lot of material to organize. Organized teachers have plenty of tricks for keeping the papers, equipment, forms, and messages from overwhelming them.

This chapter offers suggestions on getting organized and staying organized.

Don't neglect organization skills!

- Knowledge, goals, and passion are important to music education, but they become ineffective if the music educator is not organized. A music educator is often like a general running a major campaign—hundreds of students, dozens of stands, sound systems, props, scenery, music, instruments,

I came into a situation where the previous teacher wasn't very organized. The music library is a mess! So my summer plans, along with creating and updating our Web site, is to clean it out and start fresh, using my organization skills and creativity. I have requested new materials to help with this—shelving designed specifically for music libraries (crossing fingers here!) as well as boxes to file music. I also have asked for a music-office computer program to help with organization—this will help with filing and other data that needs to be kept.

I am a detail nut. Each student has an assigned folder with paper, pencil, and music in it. As they enter the room each day, they get their folder, put their stuff in an assigned spot and have a seat. If they need any extra material, it is listed on the marker board or the overhead. A schedule for the day (outline) is also listed on the marker board. Students know what I hope to accomplish the minute they enter my room. They are more focused as they see the agenda for themselves and see what I am expecting them to complete in our short amount of time. The minute the bell rings, we are warming up. After warm-ups, we take roll.

transportation, schedules—the music educator is responsible.

- I can't emphasize enough the importance of being organized for everything during the rehearsals, having the music ready to pass out, playing order on the board, along with details of future events, deadline dates, etc.

> :) I have a class walking in the door every thirty minutes with no breaks between classes. I must have all material in order with the page numbers marked so I can spend the time teaching instead of finding the correct material or page.

- There is no substitute for being prepared and organized. This not only makes teaching each day easier and more effective, but modeling these behaviors to students is also important.

- With usually a hundred students to keep track of, organization is essential in ensuring that the education of the students remains the top priority.

Organize to save time.

- Keep records, scores, and all paperwork in such order so as to permit teaching to be your primary focus.

- Staying organized saves time in the long run!

- Be as organized as possible so you don't waste the students' or your own time.

- An organized teacher is one who can free him/herself up to actually teach.

- Keep accurate records in a timely manner. Keep record-keeping tasks to a minimum so they can be done quickly and effectively.

- You can't run a good program if things are not filed and filled out correctly. You will be spending more time than needed and wasting valuable student time if things are not done right the first time and filed in an organized manner.

Have a place for everything.

- I get hard to deal with if I am looking for misplaced documents, trying to return messages late, or am not prepared for rehearsal. Organization of my space, my time, and my energy are the ways I am able to work the details of a project.

> :) By keeping my classroom orderly, by organizing teaching areas (constructing bench-type risers for singing and setting up a keyboard lab), by setting up a file system, by organizing my record keeping, and by organizing my curriculum, I have created a manageable teaching environment.

- Keep your desk clutter-free. It's hard to be a good teacher if you're not organized.

- Be organized. There is just too much going on in a music program to be sloppy about it.

- Have the room in order. Students do not like to come into an unkempt or dirty room.

- Make sure instruments are in good repair; make sure the music room is clean and that there aren't instrument cases, stacks of music, old uniforms, etc., strewn about.

Have easy access to what you need.

- An organized teacher is a happy teacher, and the students appreciate your ability to find music, folders, and information at a moment's notice.

Check out these books for more advice on how to get organized and manage your time:

- *Making Each Moment Count: Time-Savers, Tips, and Kid-Tested Strategies for the Music Class* by Cheryl Lavender ([New Berlin, WI]: Jenson Publications, 1991)

- *Teacher's Time Management Survival Kit: Ready-to-Use Techniques and Materials* by P. Susan Mamchak and Steven R. Mamchak (Englewood Cliffs, NJ: Prentice Hall, 1993)

- *Time-Saving Tips for Teachers* by Joanne C. Wachter, Clare Carhart, and Joanne C. Strohmer (Thousand Oaks, CA: Corwin Press, 2003)

- Be organized. Organization is necessary if you suddenly want to use a resource as a result of a teachable moment that suddenly becomes apparent.

- The students and parents need to know that you are in control of your administrative duties and that they can ask you questions at any time and that you will be able to answer them quickly and accurately.

I believe it is necessary to be able to access a solution to any lesson question, financial question, or concert question by referencing a file of some sort. I recently organized my lesson plans into individual manila folders—no more hunting!!

- I keep files of all the papers that I hand out. It is very easy to go back to these for information and to change dates on certain items each year.

- Keep important information for all students at each school. I have at least three copies of everything in case I am at one school and need something from another.

Keep accurate records.

- Keeping accurate records regarding grades and student progress is a must. Your mind cannot recall and remember everything.

- Be *extremely* organized. Keep incredibly detailed and current records of *everything* that goes on—absences, what was taught on what date with what

HALLE DINKLE   BY *TOM BATIUK*

class, etc. These are things I find most important so that I can stay one step ahead of the students and have proof for any dispute that may arise.

- Document! Document! Document! It makes conferences much easier.

- Records are your best friend when it comes to defending or making an important decision.

- Keeping great records of students' achievement and progress is so important. You need to be ready in case a student's parent calls you for information.

Something that will help is keeping good records and getting to know the student instead of the student being a number. Being organized helps tremendously.

> I take notes at every instrumental lesson I teach so that I can look back at their progress. I can also look up what students have missed when they are absent. I also write notes about what to cover next. It would be impossible to write specific lesson plans for each of the twenty to forty elementary groups per week.

- Cover your bases! Be prepared for any phone calls from parents or administrators about classroom and/or departmental records.

- Maintain good records of school instrument inventories, student records, and programs performed.

- Keeping good financial records, whether for fund-raising or trips or your supply budget, is important to the success of your program. It will also keep you accountable to the administration.

- Taking care of all the "non-music" responsibilities is not much fun. Keeping good records of the grades, fund-raisers, permission slips, and facility requests helps to keep a music director sane!

- Record keeping is not my strong suit, but it's extremely important to have a record of what needs to be taught again, which elements are accomplished, what drives the next lesson, what elements in the lesson require rethinking.

Stay on top of paperwork.

- Stay up-to-date with required paperwork. We all know that one of the keys to our success is the mutual respect with administration. One of the best ways to do this is to be complete and prompt with paperwork.

- Check and respond daily to voice and e-mail.

- Band directors have several roles: teacher, administrator, secretary. As soon as I get an important paper, I fill it out and send it. Otherwise it would get lost.

- Organization is a daily concentration as I keep records on students, keep lesson plans and sequences in good order, keep teaching materials in good condition and within reach during lessons, and keep up with the endless stream of paperwork, committee work, duties, and on and on.

At my age and at my career point, I have had to work harder and loosen my attitudes toward change in order to feel like I can be even close technologically to my younger colleagues. My partners are usually correct when they point out that record-keeping, grading, communications, music writing, etc., would be *much* easier and more efficient if I would just embrace a new bit of technological advancement. They are patient with helping me and are slow to say "I told you so!" when it is (repeatedly) proven they were correct.

Use technology.

- I use computers for filing, grade keeping, inventory, and more. This lets me spend more time teaching, less time doing paperwork. I also do my lesson plans on the computer, so I am building a library that is easy to access and search for future ideas. I also have used a computer during lessons, and I use the Internet to get ideas.

- Keep up with technology. My computer is my most valuable asset. I use it to keep records and do publicity items, such as posters and programs. I also use e-mail as a way to keep in touch with busy people.

- Make the computer your friend. Use it for inventory, class notes, grades, tests, biographies, student instrument information (you'd be surprised how few parents could even find a lost instrument serial #), practice records, and so on.

Delegate!

- Ideally, I could assign everything but score study and conducting to my students—and even that can be done by them! If all students have specific duties for which they are responsible, your workload is lessened and they have more ownership in the group. This even works to some extent in my general music classes.

- Delegate. Having students help you with anything they can is a big time saver.

- I have designated students who take attendance at chorus and band rehearsals. It allows me the luxury of beginning rehearsal on time, and the students are genuinely pleased to do this hum-drum chore...go figure!

- Have the students teach and lead. There is not enough time in my day to do everything myself—I call upon my students to do a great deal. This may include taking attendance, leading warm-ups, writing announcements, grading papers, filing, leading sectionals, chairing committees, and doing various other activities related to ensembles or classes.

3

"Heart
and
Soul"

Life Beyond the Classroom

Over the past several years, I have developed a "model" that I offer to students at appropriate times. The idea is to share with them some of the guiding principles I hold dear, both in and away from the musical world. After all, most of my students will not be heading off to music school or conservatory, but they will all soon be making the metamorphosis from adolescence to adulthood. It seems fitting that I give my students something they can draw on when the going gets tough. Call it a model for success, a model for fulfillment, or simply a guideline that has worked well for me. I can't say that I have held to it unfailingly, but when I sense that I am beginning to stray from its principles, I always do my best to consciously return to them.

The model for me has three basic precepts. First, be passionate. Find passion in your work, your music, and your life. In fact, go beyond passion and find a mission. Not just a job, not just a hobby, but a *mission*. The people in my life who are successful and fulfilled are filled with passion and have a sense of mission in their work, their play, and their relationships. Secondly, live with integrity. In this world, there are people who play by the rules and people who cheat, folks who lie and folks who tell the truth, those who live in the dark and those who live in the light. At the end of the day, I'd always rather be on the positive side of those statements. How else could I get a good night's sleep? Again, this seems to be a solid rule among my own role models. Thirdly, maintain balance in your life. And when the balance is out of sync, take concerted steps to fix it. It seems to me that there are seasons in our lives when we need to focus more on one area. But we must also recognize the need to feed all the parts of ourselves: our career, family life, musical soul, social life, spiritual life, and physical life. The trick is taking time to evaluate and act when one area of your life is in need of nourishment. Recently, I have found that with three young boys, my family life has required more of a prominent place in my daily activities. So I have taken action to make that happen. Have I been totally successful? Not yet, but I am trying.

This section, "Heart and Soul: Life Beyond the Classroom," addresses these issues and more. It offers concrete suggestions that address the burning question that arises in each of us from time to time: How do I find and maintain success in this career that seems to require so much time, commitment, and energy and still remain fulfilled in all the other areas of my life? You'll find valuable advice on attitude and approach, continuing education and your approach to learning, feeding your musical soul and applying your musicianship to your teaching, and your life away from school. I hope that you will find value in these tips and even stumble onto that one "nugget" you can draw on to find more fulfillment in your career as a music educator.

Scott D. Laird
Instructor of Music
North Carolina School of Science and
    Mathematics
Durham, NC

CHAPTER 5

What Personal Characteristics Do I Need?

Almost anyone who has been a student will agree that a teacher's personality influences the atmosphere of a classroom. Students may respond better to teachers with certain personal characteristics. And teachers who maintain a positive attitude may find that the classroom is more pleasant for everyone. This chapter offers insights on some of the attributes that teachers find helpful in the classroom.

Maintain a positive attitude.

- Have a good personality in the classroom. I am extremely cheerful, energetic, and funny, and I feel that is one of *the best* ways to engage students in what you are trying to teach them, especially if they come in with the attitude that they *don't* want to learn anything or that music is not important to them.

- Be friendly and positive. To quote a cliche, "You attract more flies with honey than you do with vinegar."

- Maintain a positive attitude while striving for excellence.

> Don't get discouraged. Sometimes I am not sure how much children retain until I ask them to be the teacher and I pretend to be the student. They teach just like I explained! I am pleasantly surprised at the many concepts they have remembered!
>
> All the knowledge in the world is useless if the students aren't interested. No matter what else is going on outside of the classroom, I always do my best to maintain a positive, high-energy classroom. I have beginning band students in fifth grade who practice an hour every day (a few of them before school), and I attribute this to high energy and enthusiasm.

Set students up for success by establishing procedures that the students understand and practice on a daily basis. Avoid getting on the defensive.

- Keep a positive attitude. It is important for the teacher to maintain a positive attitude toward the material to be presented and students to be taught. Griping and constant negativism destroy the purpose of the teacher...to present the best music possible in the best way possible.

- Use positive vs. negative words. Instruct using positive words. For example, "To produce a beautiful tone, it is necessary to do the following ..." versus "The sound you're producing is not very good."

- Set a good example of an educator. Our profession is starving for new teachers. Why should our students consider going into music education if all they see and hear is negative? Be enthusiastic and energetic, and encourage your students to consider music education as a career.

- There will always be issues that concern us and dominate our time. Look for the good and the positive in all that we do.

- I try to keep a positive outlook on things that are redundant to me but new to the students because of their unfamiliarity with what I am teaching.

- Keep a positive outlook. The director *is* the music program. You are the motivator for the entire program, and it is your personality and how you relate to other people that is largely responsible for the success or failure of your program.

- Keep a perspective. Things will frustrate you and make you mad. You must be able to walk away and get a new perspective.

- I maintain a positive attitude about myself. The most positive way that I can influence any situation is to first work on the one thing over which I have control—myself.

- Not only do my students know I love music, they know I love teaching. I have the greatest job in the world!

HALLE DINKLE   BY *TOM BATIUK*

> A long time ago, I started the day moving to "Bananas in Pajamas" with primary kids, and I thought, "Who else gets paid to have this kind of fun?" I call the shots, I get to decide when I stand and when I sit (and that's no small potatoes— try an office job if you don't believe me), and I get to be with kids and do all this fun stuff. It's a great way to make a living.

Be enthusiastic.

- Maintain enthusiasm about subject matter. A ho-hum, unenthusiastic presentation by any teacher does not help or encourage students to learn. We must always look for creative ways to present our subject matter.

- It takes a lot of energy to be a music teacher. But the enthusiasm you show helps to keep the students' interest level up.

- If you're not happy and enthusiastic to be in the classroom, your students won't be either.

- Enjoy what you do! You have to *sell your program* with optimism and determination.

- More than anything, I think it is important for music teachers to enjoy what they are doing. The kids will quickly get a sense of whether you like teaching or not. If they feel that you don't, then they can be quickly turned off. If they feel that you like what you are doing, then they are usually more willing to go along with you. Eventually your enthusiasm will rub off on them.

- Students really learn best by example. Teachers must have a real passion for what they are doing. However, although many have a deep passion, if this excitement cannot be shared and affect students' musical lives, no amount of passion will matter.

- A music teacher must have enthusiasm. Without it, you can't get past the fun stuff to get the students to do the hard part: to practice, to listen, and to care.

- All successful music teachers are passionate about music and music making. However, it is the passion and communication of content with our students that will always stand out as the strongest characteristic of successful educators.

- Kids can see a fraud a mile away, but they relish opportunities to work with teachers who are truly passionate about music.

- A truly effective music educator must love music. Effective music educators are passionate about music and about bringing music to students. This passion for music is contagious; I hope my students catch it!

- The best teachers I have ever had absolutely loved the subject they were teaching.

- Demonstrate a personal passion for your subject matter. Teachers must show a passion for what they teach. There is nothing that motivates a student more than seeing a motivated teacher. If teachers love what they do, it will be obvious to the students. The students will respond by pouring effort and dedication into something they are passionate about.

- You must love what you are doing! Your love and passion will shine through to the children, and they will respond in kind.

Have fun!

- Have fun! Music is a creative experience and should be enjoyable! If it's not for you, it won't be for the students either. Have fun—a good time is contagious!

- Make music fun. Music isn't "required." Don't turn it into a chore. It should be something the students want to do.

- Have fun with students. Let students occasionally choose to repeat an activity that they enjoyed.

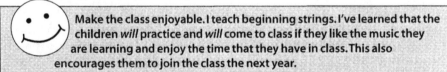

Make the class enjoyable. I teach beginning strings. I've learned that the children *will* practice and *will* come to class if they like the music they are learning and enjoy the time that they have in class. This also encourages them to join the class the next year.

Teach joy, make it engaging. If I cannot get students to love music in the elementary school, they are not going to go to the secondary schools and sign up for music. When I taught middle and high school, I would get very few students who were excited about taking music. I found that they were filled with lots of important facts, but very little of the joy of music. Consequently, I never even saw some kids because they never bothered to sign up. Later, as they learned what my classes were like, the kids would come back to music.

I use my own creativity to make learning fun. I used a few tunes from Bach and set them to words that told a story about Bach for elementary school students.

Establish traditions. We always pray (students take turns) at the beginning of each class (we are in a Christian school), and we always sing to the birthday people each month—"Happy Birthday to you...How old are you ...?" and they sing how old they are. And then they get a jelly bean for each year that they are old. And have fun. Don't be afraid to get a little crazy sometimes. When helping the children relax and sing out, we see who can open their mouth the widest and make lots of loud crazy noises and wiggles and jumps to relax and warm them up.

Make learning fun. The learning experience must be balanced between well-focused fun and relaxed hard work. Just yesterday an eleventh-grade student was exclaiming how she was amazed that she could read music, knew how to sing better, and understood about new styles of music and "didn't even know I was learning."

- Have fun teaching—*enjoy*! If the teacher does not have fun and enjoy what he or she is teaching, the program is doomed!

- Lighten up and make sure that the students know that you enjoy music and teaching.

- Have fun. Remember, kids do band and chorus to have fun. They should enjoy what they are doing and not have to struggle at it. Remember why you were in band or chorus? That feeling of pride you got from doing something well. Enjoyment can and should come from performance but also from their interactions with others in the group. Music shouldn't be a "job."

- I'm working with preschoolers, so the most important thing is that they are having fun. The best way for them to learn is to make everything a game. And I don't see anything wrong with that for any age.

- Keep learning fun for students. Be vivid in approach. Do the unexpected. Create exciting and memorable learning opportunities.

- I try to make sure music—singing, dancing, and playing instruments—is *fun* within boundaries of my room. There is freedom, but I still maintain discipline and respect and give respect to my students.

- Make it fun. Too much emphasis on perfection and discipline can be over-bearing at times.

- No matter what I am trying to teach or accomplish, I always use my creativity to make it as exciting as possible so that even the "delinquent" students will somehow be interested, take part, and feel that they may be actually learning something or at least having fun.

- Students will behave and learn better if you take your subject seriously, but don't take yourself too seriously. Everyone wants to have fun, and long-term memory is more easily established in a fun environment. Non-music teachers (whether consciously or unconsciously) sometimes convey to their students that this is their fun time. While we are having fun learning, we still must remember that there is something to be learned in the lesson. Students need to be reminded of this.

Laugh!

- Sometimes humor is the only way to get through a day and make things sane again. When used in the classroom in an appropriate way, it can really create a cooperative environment and aid in reaching the students.

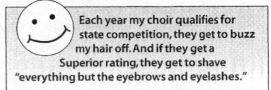
Each year my choir qualifies for state competition, they get to buzz my hair off. And if they get a Superior rating, they get to shave "everything but the eyebrows and eyelashes."

- Keep a sense of humor. I

don't know if everyone would agree that you have to be able to joke with your students or let them see you smile. This is a touchy subject. The thing is, though, you *need* a sense of humor. So maybe you don't let anyone see it. Fine. Keep it though, because you won't last six months without it.

Need a laugh? These books may have something to tickle your funny bone:

• *Better than it Sounds: A Dictionary of Humorous Musical Quotations* by David W. Barber (Toronto: Sound and Vision, 1998)
• *Ha Ha Ha Haa: Quips, Quotes, and Cartoons for Music Lovers* by Joel Rothman (London: Robson Books, 2000)
• *The Lighter Side of Teaching* by Aaron Bacall (Thousand Oaks, CA: Corwin, 2003)
• *The Teacher's Book of Wit: Quips, Quotes, and Anecdotes to Make Learning More Fun* by Mark Ortman (Kirkland, WA: Wise Owl, 1996)
• *What's So Funny about Education?* by Lou Fournier (Thousand Oaks, CA; Corwin, 2003)

• Insert humor and laughter into every lesson. Even when you teach pre-K and K, you can keep students' attention better by using silly examples and giggles! Children respond very well to silly things.

• Use humor. Laughing is so healthy.

• You can't take yourself too seriously!

• Don't forget to see life's funny moments.

• I enjoy my work and my students. However, there have been times in which strange and unplanned things happen. It is a relief to all involved if humor can be used to defuse a sensitive or uncomfortable situation.

• Use humor to get points across.

• Humor goes a long way to bridge the hard work, discipline, and delayed gratification music rehearsal requires.

• A smile and a good laugh will get you through almost anything.

Be compassionate.

• From the outset, it is important to create an unthreatening, conversational environment in which students can feel comfortable expressing themselves without fear of ridicule. Teacher characteristics include a relaxed yet confident self, a sense of humor, and an obvious optimism and enjoyment about life in general and the classroom in particular.

• Be compassionate. Everyone has an off day now and then—including me!!

- Be willing to understand each student's point of view, and be willing to take a student's situation (economic, physical, mental, etc.) into account in all dealings with the student.

- If kids can't get the concept right away, keep trying, explain in a different manner. Don't lose your temper!

Have integrity.

- Have personal integrity. *Do not ever attempt to "snow" anyone...Paybacks are @#$%!* Live the message you preach!

- Be up front with the novice musician about what will be involved in learning to read and play music, both the challenges and joys. That way, when the student experiences challenges, it will build credibility for the teacher, and the student will trust the teacher's reassurances that the challenges will be overcome with practice.

- We must be willing to listen to students and to acknowledge our own mistakes. We should never promise or threaten anything that we will not deliver on.

- Be a role model! I realize that this is a debated topic. I believe that when becoming a teacher you make a vow to be the best person you can be at all times. Your job is to teach others how to be better students, musicians, and people. The students need to see that you live a life that allows you to be a better student, musician, and person. If you place high expectations on yourself and live up to them, it will be more reasonable to place high expectations on the students, and the success rate will be raised.

- Admit mistakes or lack of knowledge. Students see right through a lie. If you make a mistake, admit it. This provides students with a role model. Everyone makes a mistake. It is important for them to learn the proper way to admit a mistake, the proper way to apologize, the proper way to correct the mistake. While you may have made a mistake in the subject, you have succeeded in teaching them a valuable character trait that will serve them the rest of their

HALLE DINKLE — BY *TOM BATIUK*

lives and also in your classroom. Students also need to know that it is okay to not be a know-it-all. While you may not know something and feel inadequate, you can know that you have succeeded in teaching the students how to handle this situation properly and helped them to see that it is knowing how to find the information that is most important. This is a skill that all employers (their future ones and your current one) are looking for in employees.

Be human.

- I bring myself to my classroom and sprinkle my teaching with my soul. My passion for music becomes their passion for music. My inspirations become their inspirations. Without expression there is no art.

- Be real, establish traditions, and have fun. Don't share every detail of your life with your students, but from time to time it is good to share a little about who you are, your family, when you were their age, a funny or encouraging story.

- I let the kids see my imperfect side too. They love it when I tell a silly story about myself that relates to what I'm teaching—they remember it forever.

- Share anecdotes about your own musical experiences.

- Learn from your students as well as teach them. When we establish ourselves as the only authority, we do not validate and encourage questioning, the making of mistakes, and other real-life ways in which we can learn.

> I view myself as an artist/musician, and I treat all my students as young musician apprentices. I want my students to think of themselves, and of me, as musicians in every endeavor in the classroom. In that way, the focus stays on developing musicianship rather than learning "about" music. The class, then, is a musical ensemble.

Be professional.

- Maintain a professional appearance and attitude. It's really easy to slip into a more casual pattern of speech and presentation at my elementary school.

- Do more than might be expected or required in order to achieve a given objective.

- Work very, very hard.

- Stay well-groomed. This is almost a joke. I believe that looking your best is always an important part of teaching. If you wear a tie and kids ask you who died, you know something is wrong.

- Respect students, parents, administrators...even if you don't wish to! Set an example of professionalism, but know and believe in your principles!

- Make the time commitment. There are two kinds of teachers: those who put in the hours needed and "beach bums."

- Keep comments professional—especially with colleagues and supervisors. You can save your gossip or other unprofessional remarks for the conversation with your spouse or close friend over a beer! Any other behavior will come back to haunt you!

CHAPTER 6

What If I Don't Know Enough?

ven the best teachers find that there's always something new to learn. Perhaps you focused your college studies on instrumental music education and now find that you are leading a choir. Perhaps the techniques that worked with your students ten years ago no longer seem to work. Perhaps you find that the students are learning, but you yourself are bored and need some inspiration. To find success, teachers must continue to be students, learning new things by reading articles and books, attending workshops, and staying connected with professional associations.

Be a lifelong student.

- The most effective teachers have a wealth of pedagogical knowledge. They continue to learn about the various instruments and better ways to teach the instruments. They continue to ferret out new ways of explaining a concept.

- Keep fresh in strategies and the art by attending workshops, taking classes, reading journals, researching materials, staying open to new things—in these ways can I better serve my students. Educators owe it to their students to keep learning, to stay mentally and musically refreshed. Educators have a responsibility to be lifelong learners.

- Keep growing. Never stop improving your teaching chops. Ask questions of pros and artists. Keep going to good seminars. Put your ego aside and just keep learning.

- Learn from others. It's important that every teacher remember to continue learning from others...be it another teacher, student teacher, or student.

- Sharpen your axe. Attend conferences, network with your peers, attend musical events. If you just keep cutting trees with the same old axe, the job will get harder and harder.

- Keeping current on new ideas, research, and best practices by master teachers helps to keep teaching from becoming routine and opens new ways to tackle old problems.

Stay up-to-date.

- I personally try to keep abreast of the current studies in education. Whether it be specific to music or general to education, I see what I can apply to my situation.

- Students do not all learn the same way; it is very important to be constantly aware of new concepts in learning theory and to apply them.

- Stay abreast of current literature. This includes purchased choral literature as well as popular listening. Students want to know that you are interested in their performance. They want to know that the literature they sing is comparable to what the other schools are singing. You need to know what the kids like and what they are hearing musically in their personal listening. Then you can talk about the vocal skills and motivate them to work on their own development.

- Keep current with new sound sources—beyond the triangle, guiro, and maracas. Rainsticks, synthesizers, donkey hoof rattles, and boomwhackers were not used when I began teaching twenty-four years ago.

- Read and keep up with the latest developments. Don't discard catalogues, read them—you don't have to buy, but you will be up on the latest in publication.

- Keep up with the current information, but don't ignore the wonderful ideas of the past.

- Keep up-to-date with teaching practices. There are almost always better ways to do things, and sometimes different strategies work for different students. I like to learn and try new ideas.

- Keep up with what's in stock at the music shop. Visit a few music shops at least once every two months. This way you keep up. You can also be proactive and order new material

- Remain awake. We are blessed with continuing education, mentors, conductors, on and on. Remain awake to what is happening in the moment— where there are opportunities to listen and learn. Be open; wonderful things are in the works if we stay awake. Read J. Palmer, read bell hooks, practice our craft.

Learn about new technologies.

- Use the latest techniques and tools available. Computers are here to stay and are a daily part of children's learning. Use them whenever possible in lesson plans. There are some wonderful CD-ROMs out there for quick access to multicultural learning.

- Whenever I need new ideas, I can usually find inspiration on the Internet through numerous professional organizations' home pages.

- By using the Internet, I can keep in contact with other teachers and see what they are doing in their classrooms. Also, the Internet provides a plethora of ideas, lesson plans, etc., that I can use in my own classroom.

> I have spent the past year educating myself on music technology and have created a Web page with MIDI accompaniments for home recorder practice and have begun to integrate composition with MIDI sequencing software into my fifth- and sixth-grade classes.
>
> I have designed a PowerPoint presentation that I use to teach an opera unit to my general music classes.

- The Internet and all the new music software out there help me to be a much better teacher.

- Keep up with music technology. This includes an emphasis on composition through the use of composition software.

- *Music K-8* has a Internet list of which I am a member. The opportunity to share ideas, joys, and concerns with other music teachers from all over the world has proved to be invaluable.

Do some research.

- Research is quite possibly the most important activity to me in my growth as a music educator. This includes reading anything that has to do with teaching music, even those materials written with band and choral directors in mind. (I'm an orchestra director.)

- Research terminology. I take the extra time to research definitions and terms used in music that are sometimes used in other subjects so that my students will have the clearest definition of the term possible as it pertains to music. I also research the simplest way of defining musical terms to young students so that they grasp the term easily.

- I research for more information than the students really need to know hoping they will be very interested and ask for more.

Read all about it!

- I read everything I can get my hands on pertaining to teaching. This helps me get ideas and suggestions to make my teaching more interesting and hopefully better.

- Due to limited time, journals allow me to read about how others might handle a situation that I have run into or am dealing with at the time.

- Read books and magazines on latest music techniques. I love reading new teaching techniques or comparing mine with other people's around the country.

- Constantly review material in the textbooks. Finding new material or a new way to present material keeps lessons fresh.

- Using professional journals has helped keep me fresh, and I have gained very useful

These publications are just sampling of the many periodicals out there for music teachers:

- *American String Teacher,* http://www.astaweb.com/
- *American Suzuki Journal,* http://www.suzuki association.org/SuzukiWeb/ASJ/ASJIndex.htm
- *The Choral Journal,* http://acdaonline.org/cj/
- *General Music Today* (online), http://www.menc.org/ publication/articles/journals.html
- *The Jazz Education Journal,* http://www.iaje.org/ journal.asp
- *Kodály Envoy,* http://oake.org/envoy/index.html
- *Music K–8,* http://www.musick8.com/
- *Music Educators Journal,* http://www.menc.org/ publication/articles/journals.html.
- *The Orff Echo,* http://www.aosa.org/echo/default.asp
- *Teaching Music,* http://www.menc.org/publication/ articles/journals.html
- *Update: Applications of Research in Music Teacher Education* (online), http://www.menc.org/publication/ articles/journals.html
- *School Band and Orchestra Magazine,* http://www.sbomagazine.com/

information from them, such as how to go about finding grant money to help fund our program.

- Subscribe to periodicals related to your area, and check publication lists for appropriate books so you can learn new ideas and ways of presentation.

- It is helpful to get trade mags and devour the information. Sometimes you just need to be reminded of what you need to do everyday.

Join professional organizations.

- I maintain my membership in the local chapter and national of Orff-Schulwerk. I attend workshops, keep in contact with colleagues, and find that those practices, although at times very difficult to maintain in my present teaching position (six schools), are extremely important to my teaching.

- I have found the ASTA online discussion group and my memberships in MENC, ASTA, and SAA to be invaluable. It's such an easy way to improve your skills and get ideas.

- Participating in my county, state, and national organizations helps me keep my

Being on the Maine Music Educators Association executive board, as member chair for three years and now as auditions chair, keeps me focused on why I belong to a professional organization. I am "in the loop." It also is a great way to stay connected with teachers across the state.

finger on the pulse of what is happening in the musical world and allows me to let my leaders know if I am happy with particular organizations' directions.

- Participate in your MEA. Local participation in your state MEA is paramount to your professional success.

The networking that you do is invaluable. The mentoring that you do and that is done for you really does make an important contribution to your music program and to the success of others teaching music.

Attend conferences.

- I'm one of three elementary band teachers in my district—and with a whopping two years experience, the most senior!!! Conferences are *vital* to my professional survival.

- Attending professional conferences is an excellent way to get rejuvenated and beat teacher burnout. It is exciting to see what other people are doing. Watching live student concerts is very inspirational as well.

- Attending conferences and workshops keeps me current, refreshes my outlook on teaching, and provides creative solutions for problem solving or scenarios I encounter at work.

- Going to any conference where a teacher can learn more about the art of music and teaching techniques will benefit the educator and the students he or she teaches. Listening to clinicians, reading new music, and sharing ideas with colleagues is essential to growing and thriving as a music educator.

- Attending state and regional conferences helps me expand my knowledge and

These are a few of the professional associations that music teachers may find helpful:
- American Choral Directors Association, http:///www.acdaonline.org
- American Orff-Schulwerk Association, http://www.aosa.org
- American String Teachers Association, http://www.astaweb.com
- International Association for Jazz Education, http://www.iaje.org
- MENC: The National Association for Music Education, http://www.menc.org
- Organization of American Kodály Educators, http://oake.org
- Suzuki Association of the Americas, http://www.suzukiassociation.org

skills and seems to always inspire me to strive for a higher standard and try new methods in the classroom.

- Go to conferences. Classes at the university are often not related to real life. I get much more from attending the annual Florida conference. It's very important to go for new music, new ideas, and relationship building.

- Attending workshops and conferences for ideas and sharing is absolutely the best way to keep up with new ideas. It's also important for one's own motivation and inspiration!

Attending MENC National in 1998 for the first time was one of the best experiences of my career! I got lots of great ideas and couldn't wait to get back in the classroom and apply what I'd learned.

I attend all sessions at our state in-service convention that deal with teaching techniques. For example, "Ten Steps to a Better Clarinet Section" was presented at the Georgia convention. It was one of the best sessions I have attended in my twenty-eight years of teaching.

- It is absolutely necessary to attend and actively participate in the many workshops that are offered for music educators. This allows me to network and share ideas with my colleagues. It also enables me to keep up with the most current methods and practices for teaching my subject area.

- In addition to regular attendance at state and county music conferences (such as NYSSMA), I try to attend a conference in an area of music that is not my specialty area. This year I attended the IAJE Conference to begin increasing my comfort in the area of jazz strings. (I'm a string educator.)

- Regularly attend Kodály workshops and national conferences. Attending divisional and national music conferences is far more enlightening than simply attending state and local conferences (and we have wonderful state and local conferences).

- Discern what is fad and what is pedagogically good for kids. It's easy to attend workshops and come back with a handful of "cutesy" ideas—I want more for my students. How does each relate to the National Standards, *and* do they really address the standards or is it a rhetorical "force fit"?

Take classes.

- Take summer workshops even if you already have forty-five credits beyond your master's degree.

- The more I learn, the more I realize I don't know. Good educators keep things green by setting new goals for themselves. Attend summer workshops—don't stop after the degrees are complete.

- Go to conferences, conventions, summer classes, and workshops. Rejuvenate yourself and remember why you became a teacher. Never settle for doing it the same every year, but always be open to new ideas and techniques that others are offering in these settings.

- It is so important to take in what you've put out over the school year. Certification in Orff, Kodály, etc., is essential to continuing the growth needed to be an effective music teacher today. I will be attending an Orff, a Kodály, John Jacobson, and an opera-writing workshop this summer as well as various music-reading sessions—I like to think of it as "recharging."

> I am a professional cellist, principal of two orchestras, and a product of the Wenatchee school district string program (traditional methods). Three years ago I began attending Suzuki institutes, and my teaching at every level (beginning through advanced) has been revolutionized, because the smallest details of technique are explored and taught with such joy.
>
> I am very fortunate to have gotten involved with the American Band College of Southern Oregon University from which I am working to get a master's degree this summer. I can attribute my improvement in teaching and approach to my teaching practice to the great lessons and professional exchange I have received in my years of attendance at ABC. I believe that if not for ABC, I would probably be in another line of work. ABC and its relevant professional development opportunity have allowed me to grow as a professional far and above any of the laughable and pathetic school-based in-services I have attended in my career.

- While I don't think it is as important which approach you choose to study, learning and using one of the current approaches (Orff, Kodály, Dalcroze, Generative, etc.) will heighten your understanding of how children learn, energize your drive to teach, and help you develop better personal music skills.

HALLE DINKLE   BY *TOM BATIUK*

HALLE DINKLE   BY TOM BATIUK

- The only way I get "charged up" for another year is to spend at least a week every summer in a professional development activity, whether it be a formal course—as it frequently is—or a seminar or workshop-type program. I know *so* many teachers who go on doing the same old thing year after year until they start thinking about retirement.

> :) It is the acquisition of Kodály certification even after many years of successful teaching that has truly helped me to be a better teacher. I feel this certification needs to become a part of undergraduate music study in all music teaching areas. What a sensible and meaningful way to learn music theory! How nice to have a teaching/learning sequence that works!

- When I take a summer school course, attend a conference, or participate in a workshop, I return to my classroom revitalized. I have new ideas to use in my teaching, and I have renewed enthusiasm for teaching. In addition to obtaining new teaching strategies, I frequently find validation for what I have been doing all along—it is good to know that I am heading in the right direction.

- Take general (nonmusic) classes to gain better perspective of general education.

- Attend classes and workshops in areas related to your teaching: conducting, Orff, Kodály, sound amplification, lighting, choreography, foreign language classes (for vocal/choral people), etc.

- Attend workshops or classes in pedagogy. Listen to the experts, and do what they tell you to do. Orff, Kodály, and Dalcroze classes always inspire me to do something new. It keeps the cobwebs off my lesson plans.

- Going back to school for my master's degree was one of the best things I could have done for myself and my students.

- Work toward advanced degrees. The learning process does not end when you graduate with the BS in education. It has only begun. I personally believe a master's program is most beneficial after you have a few years of teaching under your belt.

- Advanced degrees in music education or performance serve to keep us actively practicing what we preach to our young music students.

CHAPTER 7

How Can I Stay Musical?

Sometimes it's easy to get so caught up in teaching music that you forget about your own love of music and start to neglect your own need for musical experiences and growth. Ideally, a music teacher is both a musician and a teacher—with neither role eclipsing the other. In this chapter, teachers share how they have continued to build their own musical skills and explain why it is so important that music teachers keep up their chops.

Be a musician.

- A music teacher cannot be a successful teacher unless he or she is first a musician. Successful music teachers know their subject and must continue to practice and experience their art form.

- Remember to be a musician first. You must be a good musician *and* a good teacher to be a good music teacher. If your musicianship is lacking, you will never be able to be the best teacher you can be.

- Although there are great teachers who are not fabulous performers, and great performers who are not excellent teachers, when the two are combined it's an ideal situation. Music is a performing art, and good teachers need to

> Before teaching full time I was an accomplished orchestral and solo musician. I played principal viola and second violin in several orchestras and won the Artist International competition in 1997. I currently freelance the jobs I like in order to keep my chops up. I'm sure that being a great player helps me to be a great teacher. Teachers must model sound and technique for their students. If they don't, what will the students have to grasp onto? If the teacher's sound is weak and full of bad intonation, that is how the kids will sound. Also, the experience of playing with professionals and in professional organizations teaches teachers how to run their own groups.

know how to make good music, especially with others. The more experience one has as a performer, the more one can share with others.

- Keep up your chops. This is extremely important. Many of my students are extremely gifted and practice hours on their instruments. If I am not able to keep up with them, they don't accept my instruction as well.

- Perform in the community. It is important to get out in the community and perform as a musician so that I don't forget how to *make* music. Plus, there are many valuable nonmusic resources that can be gained through community members that I meet in these community bands.

- Keeping up skills on my instrument and performing in community music ensembles keeps me aware of where my students are headed.

- Continuing to practice your initial love and interest is key—teachers need to practice what they preach to the students that they teach. If you don't use the skills and talents you have, you might easily lose them.

- I feel that is very important to maintain your musical skills and continue to grow as a musician. The students and my colleagues are always amazed that I still take lessons and practice on a regular basis; it also sets a positive example for my students.

- Know your instrument. If you teach singing, then you'd better know how to produce a good tone.

- The old saying "those who can't do, teach" is insulting. It takes a competent musician to effectively teach music, and by continuing to perform in a community band and sing with a chorus, I have a musical outlet to keep my skills intact. Not to mention, it's *fun*!

- Participate in a music-making activity. Most of us love music and that is why we want to teach. We need to get musical satisfaction for ourselves outside of the classroom, as well as in the classroom.

I perform with our fourth- and fifth-grade shows each year. I also accompany a youth choir and teach a K–2 church choir. (I don't normally see primary kids.) For fun, I play with a steel drum band. For humility, I am working on learning trombone—because I need more bass in my band and because I want students to appreciate the difficulty for all to learn an instrument. I also play flute with a variety of groups.

Participate in the community and school as performer, patron, and conductor. I bring handbells from church to school in December and direct a staff (teachers, principal, custodian, aides) handbell ensemble that performs for the students—a big hit with students and adults. Next year, we're going to have a staff chorus perform at the talent show.

- Many aspects of teaching can be musically unsatisfying, especially in beginning-level teaching. A good performing schedule and time spent perfecting technique can fill that musical void and remind you where your students ought to be headed.

Keep learning.

- I try to take as many lessons on my primary and secondary instruments as possible. I always have something new to learn from others.

- I am a member of a brass quintet made up of fellow band directors in my area. Our weekly meetings to rehearse also are sessions on helping each other with teaching problems, ideas, etc.

- Continue to learn new music or instruments yourself. Pass on your enthusiasm!

- I take the time to study scores of pieces I will probably never conduct. This helps train my ears to hear more the advanced layers in advanced music. I find this keeps my musical mind in gear, and I'm able to memorize other scores much faster.

- Be versatile. I try and make myself a versatile music teacher by staying active in choral ensembles, playing piano, and listening to lots of different music. The more I can do, the better I can teach.

- Learning to write your own music vastly improves reading skills.

I just finished a wonderful course offered at the music school called Bodyworks for Singers. This course utilized Alexander Technique to help adults get the most out of their singing experience. Though I am not primarily a singer, I do direct an adult and a children's chorus. The insights I got from this course should help me to help my singers.

If I can't sing well using correct technique, how can I expect to teach my kids how to? Music teachers *must* continue to work on their own music technique.

I decided to play the harp after many years of piano, flute, and recorder. This experience has reemphasized the fact that learning something new is not easy. I relate more easily with my students who are just beginning recorder. It makes me much more patient with their attempts.

I participate in a yearly summer choral festival that also offers a variety of courses in areas of interest to music teachers. I am unable to sing with any groups during the school year due to time constraints with my family, and the weeklong summer festival gives me the opportunity to keep my skills sharp and to do what I love most—sing! In addition, I regularly practice the piano at home. The ability to play while maintaining eye contact with my students is a key factor in their success when learning new repertoire.

- Gain expertise in the subject. If you can't play the tuba, learn how, take lessons. Don't teach what you can't play yourself.

- Be able to relate. I still take private lessons, so on some levels I am doing the same thing that my kids are. It helps me a lot. When I'm being reminded for the third week in a row how something is supposed to be done, it helps me to remember that it takes more than one time through an explanation or a passage to get it to stick.

Use what you learn in class.

- I take lessons on various instruments and in theory to better understand what I'm conducting and working with on a piece.

- Keep the singing voice strong. The stresses of elementary school music instruction take a huge toll on the emotions, the physical body, and the voice. Voice therapy, from an intelligent and empathetic professional, makes a huge difference.

- Be able to accompany the students, especially the beginners, on a keyboard.

> Maintain your chops on everything you teach. If you teach band, be able to play the parts you expect your students to play. If for some reason you need to sit beside a student to help out or cover a part, you must be proficient enough to hold your own. A mere fifteen minutes a day on your weaker instruments should keep your chops up.

- I may not create the ultimate warm-up chorale or scale exercise, or even one that's better than those readily available. But the act of creating it causes me to ponder what I'm really trying to accomplish with the exercise. It also allows me to teach it with an enthusiasm and a deep understanding of the composer's intentions that cannot be duplicated otherwise.

- Stay aware of new trends in music in order to communicate effectively with the students.

- Become a better conductor. If I can better relate the music to my students nonverbally, they pay better attention and I can communicate with them more efficiently and effectively.

- I consider pedagogy a "chop" to keep up. I have also branched off into early music and now play recorder, shawms, rackets, etc., on a weekly basis.

- Be able to demonstrate all techniques to the student on their instrument.

Set an example.

- I think students are more willing to learn if they see their teachers learning as well. For example, I let my students know that I continue to perform and invite them to my concerts so that they can see me as a practicing musician. In addition, I share with them what challenges I face as a singer so that they know they are not alone and so that they can learn problem-solving approaches.

- Be active in outside musical activities. When students see that you are performing regularly outside of school, not only do they see that you *can* actually sing or play, but they have more respect for you for it. Students need to see that *you* practice what you preach to them, and then everything that you are trying to teach them becomes more real to them.

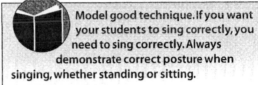

Model good technique. If you want your students to sing correctly, you need to sing correctly. Always demonstrate correct posture when singing, whether standing or sitting.

- Students will imitate your willingness to continue to improve and maintain skills. Many students think that if they, for example, know the notes, they do not need to practice. Show them how important practicing is to you.

- I feel that those who don't continue to play on some level are cheating their students of the experience of hearing someone who plays well on a daily basis. By not playing, you are sending the message that this isn't a lifetime skill and that it isn't important to continue to improve and maintain what it took years to develop.

- If my students can see me perform, then they get an idea of why practicing and performing are so important.

- As a college music educator, it is important for my students to hear me play and to realize that music is lifelong learning. It is important that they know that I still take lessons and that their musical learning does not end once they leave college and get a job.

- Kids who see or know that you perform or hear you practice will be much more apt to take your advice on their practice habits.

- I believe that it is good for the students to see you practicing and performing. It helps them to see that music can be something that continues throughout life.

Play and practice with students.

- I think it gives a good impression to the students if they see you practicing and working out licks.

- Playing my instrument with my students helps keep my chops in shape. It helps me remember fingerings and helps me realize what difficulties they may experience with their playing.

- I regularly play with the students during rehearsals and sectionals, and I especially like to play the instruments that I know the students are better at than me to show them I am human.

- Model for students "expert" performance with your voice and instrument. Don't play *with* students as often as you perform *for* students. This is how new musicians to any musical culture learn the explicit and implicit rules of a new music.

- Practice with students. My students, middle school students, will follow my exact movements. (Some even follow my facial expressions.)

- Being a trumpet player myself, I always have a trumpet by my stand at *all* times. Once students know that you can *play*, and well, their attitude and class behavior improves almost immediately. Don't hesitate to demonstrate for the kids. They like it, and I have found that it makes a *great* teaching tool.

> I play during lessons to become a role model for pitch accuracy, rhythm accuracy, tempo, etc. (I play trombone during baritone lessons and my sax during bassoon and tuba lessons... otherwise, I'm pretty much right with the kids.)
>
> I played sax with a small student combo last year. I noticed that the other sax player (twelfth grade) used many of my improv techniques! He listened, analyzed, and performed the ideas.
>
> I try to play my main instrument (trombone) and all the other instruments in front of the kids. This shows them that I am able to do so and also lets me relate to them. If I am not sure of something, I will ask their opinion since they play that particular instrument every day.

- Enjoy your own music and let it show. Students should know that you like what you are doing, and that what you do is an important part of your life. But be careful not to show your talents so much that they never get to play.

- I play along with the students. It is easier for me to demonstrate the correct way to perform a phrase or articulation than it is for me to explain the process.

- Nothing communicates the love of music or the possibilities of musical studies like the teacher performing for the students and showing them what musical knowledge can lead to.

Join a group.

- By performing, you can relate better with your performing group because you are able to sit in their chairs and evaluate the effectiveness of your director.

- Singing in a choir and cantoring at church, playing instruments in ensembles...all of these help me to be a student as well as a teacher. Being with other professionals and amateurs is humbling and gratifying.

- It's important not to forget how it feels to be on the *other* side of the baton, counting measures, getting lost, making changes in the music—all the things I expect my students to be able to do. It's important for them to know that I put myself in the same situations musically and experience the same successes and problems they do.

- I regularly sit on the other side of the baton. The benefits: I learn new literature, keep up my chops, build relationships with other musicians, and supplement my teaching salary! It is so fulfilling after a day of teaching to sit in an orchestra and play good music myself.

Performing consistently helps me discover new ways to help my instrumental music students overcome their own performance problems. Also, they enjoy hearing my performance anecdotes, as it brings them into the real world of music, and they realize that making music is a lifetime activity.

I sing with the Cleveland Orchestra Chorus. As a choral director, I believe this helps me be a better teacher. I realize how tedious rehearsals can get if you are just sitting waiting for another section to learn something. I try to keep that in mind when I am rehearsing my students.

I play in a rock band and purposely book engagements that my students can attend so they can see me in a different light.

I find that although my K–7 students create some fine things, I still thirst for more. I play French horn with a semiprofessional orchestra, and I feel that this provides me with the best of both worlds.

- It's really important to continue making music. Remember, the joy of making music is probably what inspired you to become a music educator in the first place. Don't get so wrapped up in teaching music that you don't make the time to participate in musical groups. You could be in church groups or community groups. Also, don't just be the leader. It's great fun to be one of the "kids" again! Be *in* the bell choir, as opposed to directing it!

- The ability to perform keeps the love alive. Sometimes one gets tired of continually teaching and not having the ability to do things oneself.

- I learn so much while playing. Many of the techniques that I have heard my conductor use, I take back to my rehearsals and use with my students. In addition, I am constantly learning something new about music.

Listen.

- Listen, listen, listen. This is more important than keeping my chops up for two reasons: (1) I listen to expose myself to other interpretations of music I am currently working on and to stay current with recordings and new works for my groups. (2) I listen to just plain great music whenever I can. It helps me stay

HALLE DINKLE BY *TOM BATIUK*

focused and energized, especially at the end of the year. Piano music is my favorite.

- I listen to as much music as I can. This would include watching MTV, attending the theater, and attending university performances and concerts at other high schools.

- Go to as many different styles of concerts as possible. Keep an open mind to new music styles, arrangements, and instruments.

- I believe it is important to participate in *live*, quality performances solely as a listener so that I am not distracted by active participation. I cannot expect my students to attend concerts to learn if I am not willing to do the same.

- Listen to concerts "great and small." Get your "ears" out of your classroom and stay exposed to professional music performances within your idiom, and otherwise. Also, go to big conferences and listen to fine groups of kids like yours.

- Attend live performances of groups at the level of your students and above. Listen to performance recordings and demo recordings so you can provide a variety of literature for the students in your performing ensembles, including "challenge" pieces that encourage them to grow and improve.

- Listen to other bands at contests. When I hear a really great band, it inspires me to work toward that level of performance with my students. Hearing the band seems to provide me with a reality check on what is truly possible with the age group that I teach.

- I listen to recordings of music I will do and music my high school group will never do so I know what's out there and what good groups should sound like.

- I listen to a large number of CDs, and I record my band to listen to my students. It keeps my ear in shape and reminds me of the importance of efficient rehearsals.

- I try to keep my musical horizons open by listening to all of the popular music of the current time. There are many popular songs that are based on (or have similar characteristics to) some well-known classics.

- Keep up on the newest music styles. This way I am able to use what my students listen to as a tool for teaching music instead of using outdated material and artists. This helps to show the students that their music is fun and educational, and it keeps their interest.

- Stay on top of today's current musical trends. Being aware of the current listening of my students helps me to teach basic techniques of rhythm and melody in language they understand.

CHAPTER 8

How Can I Take Care of My Needs?

N o one works well when physically, mentally, or emotionally exhausted—and music education is one field where it's easy to exhaust yourself. The demands of preparing lessons, planning concerts, practicing your own music, communicating with parents, and everything else you have to do can drain you of all your energy, making it difficult to manage any of your responsibilities. Many teachers have found that they must work hard to achieve balance in their lives. They take time for family, friends, fun, exercise, and rest. By taking these steps to achieve balance in their lives, they find that they can bring more energy back to the classroom.

Maintain personal balance.

- Maintaining personal balance is essential for keeping your stress levels in check. A stressed-out person can find it very difficult to be an effective educator.

- Without personal balance, I would burn out. I need to take time for myself in order to refresh my mind and body.

- Abraham Maslow states in his "hierarchy of needs" that there are certain personal requirements (physiological, safety, love and acceptance, self-esteem) that must be met before self-actualization can occur. My priorities must be in check so that I do not burn out, get frustrated, or not want to do my best for the kids.

- When I am unhappy before and after school, I tend to be more stressed at school. I can't say that I have achieved a balance, but my twelve-hour days are not as common as they were a year ago.

- Though I feel I still put in the long hours necessary to do the job right, I have learned to acquire more personal balance so that my teaching can be excellent. I have changed my eating and health regimen, made efforts to have a life and interests outside of music, play in music groups for my own satisfaction so that ten, fifteen, or twenty years from now, I will be able to deliver the same quality teaching I deliver today.

Have a life outside school.

- It's a job, not a lifestyle. We tend to become music educators twenty-four hours a day, and it takes over our lives. It would be healthier if we could learn to turn it off sometimes!

- Leave your work at work and your home life at home. Bringing things to school or even carrying things over class to class can have a negative effect on your teaching. Also, take time at home with your family—after all, they should come first.

- If you eat, sleep, and drink teaching twenty-four hours a day, seven days a week, you aren't doing your students any favors. All teachers need to find a happy balance between their personal lives and school. By achieving that balance, teachers will act as excellent models of how a healthy adult should be. If you concentrate intensely on school all the time, you will burn out easily.

With a twenty-five-year perspective, I think I can speak with some authority when I say that teaching is one of the most difficult jobs on God's green earth! I firmly believe that this profession will consume a person who doesn't have a solid awareness of "life balance." Reassessing personal priorities should be an ongoing practice for everyone, especially those of us in education. If personal priorities are not in order, emotional and physical burnout is inevitable. Here are my priorities at this point: wife, children, extended family, self-interests, colleagues, job and church. This seems to be an honest assessment of how my decision hierarchy exists at the present. Examples: If I have a concert at school, but I have sick out-of-town relatives needing my help, I defer to my family. If I have a meeting as part of my responsibilities on professional boards and my daughter has a performance, I go to my daughter's concert. If church choir is scheduled the same time as a rehearsal for the community choir I sing with, I attend the community choir.

Personal balance is something I didn't have during my first year of teaching, and I was very burnt out by the end of the year. I try to take time for martial arts, bicycling, reading, cross-stitch, etc. I read for ten minutes before I go to sleep at night so I don't always fall asleep thinking about school.

Let students know that music is a vital part of life, but not the only part of life; teach balance. I teach in a small school and find that my students are all in every activity. My best band students are also the starters on the basketball team and the leaders of every other activity in the building. We often talk about life balance and fitting it all in without compromising our own well-being.

- I could work twenty-four hours a day being a music educator and not get everything finished. In fact, it will never be "finished." Making sure I have time for my family and personal time in pursuits of my own (unrelated to music) helps me keep a balance in my life that makes me a better teacher.

- You can so easily become burnt out if you don't do something outside of school. It is much easier to keep a positive attitude and a good rapport with students and staff if you can leave school behind on occasion.

- If I don't have a life outside of my job, how can I teach children to be healthy adults?

I do my work at school, during school hours. I tend to dawdle when given an unlimited amount of time. Over the years, my husband has shown me that I can get just as much done during the school day as when I stay late. He's right!

Through my anecdotes in the classroom, students know I have a life beyond the classroom. My health is important, and so I look for opportunities to keep active and expand my mind in many other areas. Every time I try something new, it improves my teaching abilities!

Spending time doing something other than music is a great relief. Personally, I like to walk with my wife and talk about things important to her. This gets my mind off the intonation of clarinets and the fact that the percussion section all got referrals from the substitute teacher for playing the drums. I am also into the martial arts, which keeps me physically in shape and gives me a release for frustration.

- If you are unable to walk away from your job at the end of the day and revive your spirits, you will end up edgy and unable to relate to your students who live lives outside of the music classroom.

- Know when to take a break. You can never get everything done. Know when to put the work down and have quality time with family and friends.

- No one individual is irreplaceable. Not even you! Take time to walk, exercise, plant a garden, talk to your dog or cat, etc. (If your cat seems

HALLE DINKLE   BY TOM BATIUK

to be more attentive to your banter then your students, then it is time for a vacation.)

Make time for yourself.

- I take time for myself. This is so important. It enables me to rejuvenate and become a more rested and in-control person. Students take a lot of energy!

- I set boundaries with my time and use of my talents. If I don't learn to say no, I will get burned out.

- Planning for "me" time is so important for a busy teacher. Often, this needs to be planned and enforced.

- Make time for yourself daily. Do something that *you* like to do that is completely different from teaching to refresh your spirits and ease your mind.

- Don't get so caught up in school that you have no other activities just for you.

I take a walk every night after school. I need down time to get my mind off of school for thirty minutes. I also play in small community bands, which allows me to keep my skills up and is relaxing because I don't get to perform in school.

Take a break. I use running, hiking, roller-blading, or whatever to clear my mind and have a change of pace so that what I am teaching can be exciting to both myself and my students, and so that I remain positive and balanced myself.

I find if I spend at least thirty minutes each day in mindful meditation, being in the moment, my class experience is much calmer and more productive.

- I take time out of each day (at least ten minutes) to decompress and do whatever I want to do!

- I take time to walk in the evening or in the park on the weekend. Also, my husband and I attend orchestra concerts and musicals as often as possible to refresh the soul.

- I pray every day—I can't do this alone.

- Find some time for silence every day. It's a noisy world. It's hard to hear the inner voice. Silence helps.

Stay healthy.

- Maintain health. Poor job attendance affects student learning. Lack of sleep affects teacher judgment in reacting to students' behavior and questions.

- I keep my energy up by drinking water. If I'm not energetic, the kids pick up on it and are all over the place.

- Plenty of rest to maintain good health is a necessity for me. I strive to get at least eight hours of sleep each night. This usually prevents excessive illness during the year and provides the energy level I need to be consistently "on my game" at school.

- You need time away from your job to keep your body and mind healthy. Exercising and keeping a healthy diet will not only improve your persona, but will improve your focus and give you the energy you need to keep on top of things.

- I teach K–12 instrumental and vocal music at a school of about four hundred students. The daily schedule isn't too terrible, but finding music to perform for concerts, etc., is a job that is unbelievable. One has to keep healthy physically and mentally in order to keep things together.

- Feeling rested and strong with proper nutrition and exercise helps me maintain a sense of well-being. Fatigue and a feeling of weakness or illness hinder teachers from doing their best.

- I de-stress after school. I try to work out at my health club four times a week. It clears my head and gets rid of stress.

- Being a band director takes up a huge amount of time and energy. I have to keep myself in good health (mental, physical, and emotional), or I know that my body will shut down and I will be sick. I try to exercise every day and eat well. When I'm on the run, that's not always easy.

- If you do not stay healthy inside and outside, you do more harm than good for yourself, family, school, and, most of all, your students. It's hard to keep a balance; you must constantly work at it.

- Keep fit in body and in spirit. You can't be at your best with the kids if you don't feel good about all aspects of yourself. If you don't feel good, you can't give your best to the students, so you need to be healthy and in good mental condition.

Take time for family and friends.

- This is a job; your family is the most important thing.

- Eating right, getting proper rest, being organized, and having other interests all

My first year at my school, I noticed that very few people went to the volleyball games. I love volleyball, so I went to as many as I could. Two years later, the coach asked me if I would like to be the team's line judge for their home games and one or two close-by away games. I heartily agreed and performed this labor of love for that year and all of the following. The team members became very good students in my classes. The fact that I was supporting them in something they loved to do that was nonmusical really seemed to touch them, and they showed support to me in things that are musical. Now I'm the assistant volleyball coach at our school and loving every minute of it. Oh, and now, I relate many musical things to volleyball. You'd be surprised how well music and volleyball mirror each other, and mirror life.

HALLE DINKLE   BY *TOM BATIUK*

contribute to the well-being of an individual. It is a juggling act sometimes to fit it all in, but just working long hours can ruin a person's health and family life. Always put your own family first as much as you can. They will, in turn, support what you do.

- Keep the peace at home with friends and family. My family and social life are my greatest support. Staying connected with family and friends makes life, life.

- Set aside time for family. While music teaching can be all-encompassing and time-consuming, set aside time for your family that will not be violated by those activities. You'll approach your job with freshness, and your family will benefit from the attention.

- Take advantage of prep time at school. By taking full advantage of time given at school (not going to custodian's room, cafeteria, etc.), I am able to go home to be with family at a reasonable time.

- I keep in touch with my kids—playing, reading, hugging—and keep in touch with my honey—talking, playing, hugging.

Have a hobby.

- Just as we advocate that students need a well-rounded education, we too need to be well-rounded in our lives.

- It is refreshing to engage in a favorite pastime outside of the classroom. It's also necessary for our students to observe that we are well-rounded.

- Try to maintain a balance in your

I travel to venues where the culture is different from my own. This has always broadened my horizon and given me new perspectives upon which to expand teaching approaches and ideas. For examples, my travels to Indonesia led me to learn to play gamelan.

I feel I am a better teacher because I don't spend my whole life in this little part of the world. I have learned customs, inflections of speech and behavior, dances, and stories that I can use to explain and inform what I teach. Having been many places, I don't find music from exotic locales to be as odd sounding as my students do.

life by pursuing your own talents and hobbies outside music. You will energize your spirit and keep your brain activated in these other pursuits, and this practice will prevent burnout and will broaden your knowledge and perspective.

- Music is a very intense, high-profile, high-burnout profession. If I don't care for myself, I will not be able to continue what I do with exuberance and joy as I do now. As the year ends with exhaustion with more parties and performances, I look forward to skiing, eating healthy, exercising, and writing music.

- Do something other than music for recreation! Be multidimensional! We are only as shallow as we restrict ourselves to being.

- Have a hobby that is not musical. Do something...and don't think about work. Have other interests and, more importantly, socialize with people who are not in your profession.

4

"People"

Personal Relationships

Success or failure in teaching is rarely a reflection of pedagogical preparation, but of quality of the relationships with all stakeholders. For music educators, musical skill and knowledge are mostly tangible attributes acquired with substantial practice and study. Quality personal relationships and interactions are not as easily defined. Successful teaching requires strong relationships with children, parents, administrators, and clerical/custodial staff, as well as a strong sense of inner peace. We will all spend our lifetimes striving for healthy interactions in all of these areas. As the years march on, my long list of guiding principles continues to expand as I work to nurture these relationships.

What is best for kids should be the litmus test for any decision made during the teaching day. Kids want and need boundaries, guidance, and the knowledge that you care about them. The quote, "They may not remember what you teach, but they will remember how you treat them," rings true.

Too often, our first interaction with a parent is to give a negative message about student work or behavior, which starts us on the wrong foot. Seek out opportunities to meet with parents in a positive, non-threatening environment, thus providing a foundation for further dialogue. Support comes more quickly when you are asking it of someone with whom you have a positive history.

Too often we strive to know the names of our new students but have a hard time naming all of the adults in the building in which we teach. As music educators, we have a tendency to ask a great deal of these adults. Whether it relates to scheduling, facility use, or pulling kids out of other classes, too often, the question is, "What can they do for us?" These folks can quickly become extended family as we share our lives over the years. Invest time and energy in these adult relationships. Spend time in the faculty lounge, and organize or attend social events. Offer as much help to colleagues as you ask of them. A handwritten letter of appreciation should be as routine as a requisition form.

The relationships that need the most care are immediate. As teachers, we often provide for our classroom at the expense of those around us, including ourselves. We are most successful as teachers when we have taken care of ourselves and nurtured the relationships with those dearest to us.

Education is under siege from the national to the local level. Funding is down and privatization is on the agenda. We are asked to do so much more with so much less. This said, we are crusaders in the noblest of professions. At the end of the day, unlike so many others who are "working to make a living," we are able to say that our work will have an infinite effect on thousands of lives. We change lives and open minds, doors of opportunity, and windows to what can be. For this we have extreme wealth.

Read on for additional insight into how we can build better relationships with those who come in contact with us and our music programs.

Brett Smith
Music Teacher
O. H. Anderson Elementary School
Mahtomedi, MN

CHAPTER 9

How Can I Build Better Relationships with My Students?

Students are, of course, a huge part of every music classroom. Having a good relationship with students is key to having a successful program. Knowing your students, caring about them, and treating them with respect can make your day—and your students' day—brighter and can make the rehearsal or lesson more pleasant and productive for everyone.

In this chapter, teachers share their suggestions for building great student-teacher relationships.

Put students first.

- Put the students first! Teachers should place the students' needs before their own. The teacher's job is to help each student develop as a student, musician, and person. In order to do this, the instruction must be student centered. Teachers must use their own expertise, creativity, and knowledge to create a curriculum that teaches the National Standards while meeting the needs of students as individuals.

- Make certain that the kids know that they are the most important. While I teach band, the kids would not be as open and desiring to learn an instrument as they are if they didn't think that they were the most important. I teach kids first—band second.

- In rehearsal situations, I continually ask what I would be feeling were I playing in the group.

- Remember the kids are why we teach. Keep your ego out of the job.

- Make the kids your first priority. Base all decisions that you make regarding your program on the needs of your students.

- Always remember the students. The kids come first. I'm teaching children through music, not music to children. I want to change their lives and bring beauty to their world.

Treat students with respect.

- Students need to be treated as though they are real people, not second-class human beings.

- Teenage students have thoughts, emotions, good days, bad days—just like adults (only magnified!). By tuning in to and respecting these things, I can honor them. Then we can learn music, some days "in spite of," and some days "because of," what's going on in our lives.

- You must care about the students as individuals. This does not mean getting involved in their personal lives. It means thinking of them as people and not just as cogs in your band machine.

- It never occurs to me to order a student around, no matter what he or she has said or done. I have found that "Please" and "Thank you" are especially important when I'd least prefer to use them with an errant student.

- Focus on respecting the students. Try to work with students instead of insisting on only one way to deal with them. Smile and be kind even when remaining firm on issues that may be negative.

- Always remember that we are dealing with people, not objects or things. Our rooms must always be a safe place where we can all try without the fear of failure.

- Respect students' taste! Taste in music can change only if we can get students to try a bite! They never will if you put their music down!

- Don't try to be a buddy to your students. You need to be friendly and establish

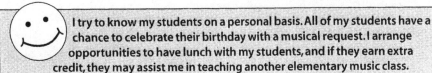

I try to know my students on a personal basis. All of my students have a chance to celebrate their birthday with a musical request. I arrange opportunities to have lunch with my students, and if they earn extra credit, they may assist me in teaching another elementary music class.

Meet the students at the door. As my young teenagers enter the band room each day, I personally greet as many as I can. We talk about how their lives are going—did they get a hit in baseball last night, what rock concert did they go to, what are they listening to on the radio or Internet? It makes all of us more human.

good student-teacher relationships. You need to earn the respect of your students. If you do, this will carry on for years.

Be caring.

- When students know that you care, they also will care. When they believe that you will do what you say you will do, then they will trust you and give you all they have.

My door is always open to any student who needs to talk to me. I listen and try to give advice without trying to sound "preachy." There are some serious problems being faced by these students, and sometimes they just need to know that there is someone who cares whether or not they succeed. You don't have to be their best friend—they already have one of those. I still have alumni come to me and talk about what they are going through in their lives. Trust is a very important tool for a teacher. Earn it.

When one of my kids happens to be having a particularly rough day (I have several with terminally ill parents), it is so gratifying to see fellow students reach out to be compassionate. I allow this within certain time constraints and situations and find that, sometimes, the best medicine is a hug or even a group hug (depending on the class). It builds our humanity as a group and somehow gives the performance of our music even more depth.

- Show kids you care. My experience has been that the more I attend events students are involved in, make phone calls home to parents for *any* reason, ask them about their lives and interests, the harder they work for me and the better they play.

- If you care for your students, attitudes will be more pleasant, you will find each other more credible, and all of you will enjoy the time together much more than if you do not care for them.

- I make it a point to know every student and family. My band kids spend more time with me than any other teacher. We not only make music, but we are very much together like a family. To many students, I am the father figure; to many others, I am a second father. This relationship demands that I be available to counsel them as well as rehearse the ensemble. I think my kids know that I am here for them. It works for me. If you don't like kids, don't teach.

- Children will go beyond themselves if they love you and know you love them.

Enjoy the students.

- By enjoying and respecting the children in my care, I can genuinely share with them my love for music in the hopes that they may love it too, and thus music may enrich their lives more fully.

- I delight in students and always try to enjoy the idiosyncrasies of the age group that I'm teaching and appreciate what makes these kids tick.

- Enjoy the presence of students in the classroom. They know if we are happy to see them. That's most of the battle; all beings need to love and be loved.

- I try to bring a simple little bit of fun in the interaction between me and the students. For example, when a student says something that is cute or interesting, I might put my hand on my forehead and exclaim, "I can't believe my students say those things!"

Be encouraging.

- You need to motivate the students, and in order to do that, you need to encourage them by being supportive. Do not give compliments until they deserve them. Give them something to work toward. Let them know that you respect them and care for them and their successes and failures.

- Help others to feel good about themselves, and they will feel good about you.

- I encourage novices in their strong points and help them to correct faults. Encouragement is important, but falsehoods, telling them they are good when they are not, do not help them improve. One teacher I knew did this; they were very embarrassed when they performed at a contest and received the lowest rating possible.

- Frequently recognize student accomplishments. I like to include not only musical accomplishments but also any athletic or academic accomplishments. It uplifts all of us to hear a student play a solo he or she has been working on, or to hear about the successful youth orchestra audition, or making the A honor roll, or making the basketball team, etc.

- "I can't" is a dirty word in my classrooms. The pressure is on me to show students how to. *Then,* the pressure is on them to take it and work with it. We teach students how to practice—and to help them learn they can do *anything* from the inside out. Have them say "yes, I can" to you in the hall instead of "Hello Mr. or Ms.," and they will start to believe it in most areas of their lives.

- Kids in my room may not say "I can't." I have a poster in my room that says, "Success comes in 'cans' not in 'can nots.'" If kids believe they can, they have success.

- Using compliments more than criticism will help students feel good about themselves. You can get almost any point across in a positive manner with the same results.

- A bulletin board of articles from the paper, advertiser, or school newsletter, along with programs and pictures, gives a feeling of pride for those who participate. They work harder and pull the others along.

Correct when necessary, but always stay positive. When we are negative to our students, we are speaking self-fulfilling prophecies. I tried staying positive a couple of years ago with my eighth-grade chorus, and the results were amazing! This was the best sound I'd had in four or five years. I unfortunately did not try it with one of my high school choirs that same year, and by the end of the year, the younger group was the better of the two. We can make or break our own programs by correcting mistakes made, yes, but also by building positive experiences wherever and whenever possible. Compliment on a good attribute, then offer solutions for making it (or another) better.

Have an awards/recognition policy. Our music department has a yearly music awards night to recognize all the hard work our students have done over the course of the year. It has kept our students active, interested, and proud of their accomplishments.

- Praise students frequently when they are trying to achieve success. Encourage students to *try* what may appear to be difficult. Even when they show minimal success, it's important to praise with enthusiasm. Use words such as "Great job! Try that again," "I knew you could do it!" or simply "That's it!" "You did it!" or "Keep up the great work!"

Give them ownership.

- Encourage students to make music their own. When children learn to read, they learn to write and develop their style of ownership. Music students need to learn to create their own music.

- If we, as educators, can find a way for our groups to own the program, discipline originates from the inside out instead of the outside in.

- Give smaller music groups some choice in music performed. This gives them a sense of ownership. Not all judges approve of their choices, but this is part of the learning process.

- When children become completely involved in the teaching process, then the outcomes are generally more satisfying to all. For example, a simple talent show requires a good director, lighting coordinator, music operator, curtain person, stage crew, and a group of talented performers. Total class participation!

- I use a survey at the beginning of each new semester class to assess students' interests, background, and understanding. Effective communication is at least a two-way process, and learning about the receivers helps to facilitate the teaching/learning process.

- Make the students have ownership of their program. If it is the teacher's choir, then the only person who really cares is the teacher.

- Ask the students for feedback. At first, they won't think you really want an answer, but if you accept the first answers, you will get more in-depth ones as

they feel more comfortable. I ask for feedback on music we learned, how my conducting comes across, what they felt about their performance, etc.

- If possible, establish a Big Brother/Big Sister policy between high school band and elementary feeder schools. Incorporate lessons given by the high school students and even social activities to promote recruitment.

Listen.

- No matter what, I try to listen, within reason, to what my students have to say. We have journal time, which gives them a chance to reflect on their learning and gives me feedback on how well they are grasping the concepts.

- Be a considerate and respectful educator. Be willing to understand each student's point of view, and be willing to take a student's situation (economic, physical, mental, etc.) into account in all dealings with the student.

- Sometimes a willing ear and a closed mouth are the best recipe for a teacher. By listening to students' needs, a teacher can better prepare daily lessons to encourage social development, as well as development of musical skills.

- Picture this: A three-year old teaching the thirty-five-year-old a song. Elizabeth taught me the second verse to "Twinkle, Twinkle, Little Star" in the stairwell of our school. (Actually, she sang it to my stuffed bunny, Ravel.)

- Take time to listen to your students. Some days you may be the only adult in your students' lives that they will talk to. Take the time to listen (and not always about the music)!

- I teach better with open ears, not an open mouth. The better that I listen to my students musically and verbally, the better, clearer, and *faster* I can present solutions to them. As a teacher, I need to listen in order to know why my students are participating in my program. I need to know, for instance, if children are there because Mom says so or because they love to express themselves through music. It makes a difference in presentation of the lesson so that the student who at the beginning of the year was forced to play may *want* to continue.

Get to know them.

- Show interest in each student. Most students who feel the teacher considers them more than just a body in their classroom will be more productive.

- Be personal. Make eye contact with each child at some point during the class.

- Learn children's names quickly. It helps if they know you know who they are—I use name games at first. Seating charts help too.

- No matter how many students you have, make sure you know their names, families, and at least one nonmusical interest of each student.

- Know your students, be sensitive to their learning style, their musical background and needs, and their family background when it affects their learning and behavior, and continually challenge them in such a way that they thirst for more!

- I find it extremely important to communicate with students about their musical likings. In addition, I think it is very important to get to know the students' personalities in order to best communicate your ideas with the students. Since students' personalities affect the way they learn, it is important to seek needs the students have in order to fully teach the students. Also, knowing their perspective about situations in class or at rehearsal or about life in general helps you to modify teaching practices for the student or the class.

I have my students fill out surveys at the beginning of each year. Some of the questions ask what other activities they are involved with. I attend the majority of the sporting events, plays, recitals, etc., that my students are involved in. I also go to some of their church performances when I can. Seeing me at their other activities builds a bond that can carry into my classroom. Students work harder for me if they believe I care about them as people. (And I do.) I think that I am there to help them develop as a complete people, not just as musicians.

Talk to the students outside of class on a more personal basis. Find out what's going on in their lives. One of my seventh graders couldn't seem to stay awake in class where before he was very much "with it." I found out that his mom had just had twins, and the babies' room was right next door to his.

- Take time to get to know each student. It's easy to miss students when there are so many going in and out of your room each day. Make a point to at least say hello to each student during the course of a week, and take time to ask them how things are going. It's also a good idea to keep track of this so you don't miss a single student. This also helps to make them feel like an essential part of the ensemble.

Learn about their nonmusical lives.

- It is important to know what is important to your students, not just while they are in your class, but in other aspects of their lives.

- Keep in contact with students after they leave elementary school. I continue to attend their concerts, plays, sporting events, graduations, and weddings.

- Get to know the students well in different aspects of their lives in order to understand where they are coming from, where they need to go, and how to help them more effectively.

- It is important that your students know that you care about what else they are involved with in their lives besides band, orchestra, or choir. My community service involves constantly supporting my students with my presence at their sporting events, scout inductions, recitals, or church functions. It means a lot to your students, and the rewards to your ensembles are priceless.

> Keep in touch with current student interests. Students are always amazed that I listen to some of the same music they do, not just classical music all the time. When I can quote pop songs or artists, they feel a type of comfort level—it's strange how it works—but they love knowing that I relate to them on their level.
>
> Keep up with current trends in music and other areas of interest of the students. I'm over sixty, but I do know what March Madness is, as do all of the students, especially boys. I mentioned that term to our new (elderly) superintendent—he had no idea what it was.

- Check up on academic growth of students and stress the importance of having a good academic background.

- Many of my students don't practice. Many instruments don't even go home. (Parents have pawned school instruments in the past!) So, I need to be aware of the situations at home before getting on some students about their practice time. Written and listening assignments are more effective for these students.

- Have knowledge of students' lives outside the classroom. My students tend to respect me more and confide in me more when I know *who* they are and what makes them who they are.

Keep up with the times.

- Have students tell you why they listen to the music they do. What makes them listen to certain styles of music sometimes can be the same reason they eat what they do or wear what they do or even act how they do. Sometimes I find it better to work backwards from today's music rather than to jump to a certain period and expect students to dive right into something they don't understand or even care to.

- Being aware of what my students are "into" helps me to communicate with them.

- I try to stay somewhat current with the music kids like to listen to, even though their music may drive me crazy!

- Keep up-to-date with the music groups of the times. I teach high school guitar and have found it helpful (though painful at times) to listen to what the kids are listening to. I try to get inside their heads and go where they are. It's not always a good place, either.

- Pay attention to student behavior with friends to understand their culture and attitudes.

- Keep current with kid culture. Students need to know that their musical affinities are valid and respected.

Know child development.

- Know the developmentally appropriate practices for the age level you teach, especially if you change grade levels during the day.

- Know how to deal with and speak to youngsters. You've got to talk their language and understand that they sometimes have a different way of perceiving ideas.

> In order to teach any age group most effectively, one must understand what and how much any given age group is truly able to understand, internalize, assimilate, and demonstrate. For example, when teaching rhythms, most of us were taught to present the fractional rhythmic pyramid (whole note = two half notes, half note = two quarter notes, etc.). When I learned two things—(1) that most learners do not possess the capacity to truly understand fractional concepts until around the age of twelve or thirteen and (2) that most children learn reading first by recognizing "sight words"—I had much more success teaching developing band students rhythmic reading by approaching it with the concept of recognizing "rhythmic chunks."

- Know what the students need. I make sure I know where the students are, where they want to go, and where they need to go. Then we can figure out how to get there.

- In order to teach effectively, we must continually be aware of the students' developmental status and goals.

- Be able to relate to the children you are teaching and know what they need.

Children will respond better to you if you understand their needs and you don't expect more than they are able to learn at their level. They want to be loved and accepted, but challenged also.

HALLE DINKLE

BY *TOM BATIUK*

Know the school population.

- Be realistic about your venue. For example, if you are working in areas where the families are financially at a disadvantage, don't demand private lessons. They are trying to keep food on the table and a roof over them.

- Consider the school population. Are they low or high socioeconomically? My approach to the students changes considering this.

- I am in an area of many Native American students. I feel that learning more about their cultural background has aided me in understanding and teaching them.

Allow for differences.

- Treating students as individuals is important. It's easier to see a class as a unit, rather than taking the time to think about each individual students' needs and abilities.

- Take a personal interest in students. Be aware that students are not all alike and that they have individual needs and styles.

- Allow the students to be themselves. Different students learn differently.

- Individualize music instruction. Be aware of learning styles, interests, and abilities of your students and be flexible.

- Appeal to a variety of students. Attempt to show all students that music has an impact in their lives every day and make them aware of the influence of the arts on their development. Encourage participation by all students in musical groups, even special needs students.

- Teach respect for other students. All students are the same regardless of race, individual appearance, economic background.

Spend time with them.

- Work with students after school. In addition to extra after-school rehearsals for my choruses, I often work with particularly talented students for solo parts,

> I find it essential to treat my students with respect and dignity. This is crucial to having a well-behaved class. One thing that I do is to try to make it down to the cafeteria once or twice a week to sit down and eat lunch with them rather than eating with one hand and typing on my computer with the other worrying about the things I need to get done. Making kids feel like they are special to you is much more important than that list of things to do. I also like to know about something they do outside of band and ask them about it on occasion.

Teach the student before the family. Over the years, I've had more success with students who are at risk when I don't know that they have the label. In new schools, I've had colleagues try to tell me who to "watch out for" due to family problems, wealth (or lack of), etc. I do try to read up on IEPs, but I try to incorporate the expectations within the whole group, not just singling out someone.

accompaniment, or instrument ensembles to complement my choruses.

- Outside of class time, student contact (lunchroom, hallways) can be informative. Students will let you know what they liked, disliked, and want to do more of in this kind of informal setting, away from the pressures of the classroom.

- Eat with your students if possible on a regular basis in your room. You get to know them on a more personal level, and when it comes to crunch time they are there for you.

- Eat lunch with students occasionally and get to know them! Kids are more willing to work if they know you and understand you (to a reasonable degree).

- Spend time with kids outside the classroom. I try and spend time with my students outside the classroom at sporting events, picnics, concerts, etc.

Don't forget anyone!

- Notice every student and establish eye contact. When dealing with large performing ensembles, it is difficult but essential to make sure every student feels acknowledged. Many of the quieter or less "talented" children are never "seen" during the school day, and when people feel visible they tend to feel included and contribute more.

- Include *all* students in instrumental music. Students who are in inclusion classes or on IEPs can successfully participate in practically all aspects of an instrumental music program. But it is work for the educator. Music must be rewritten or transcribed to meet the needs of the slower learner.

- Include everyone. Few students are totally tone-deaf. Encouragement and nurturing produce tremendous results. I try to let as many students as possible participate in performance ensembles, concerts, plays, and classroom activities. This has revealed unexpected talents in a few students who would have fallen through the cracks.

- Check on the students who are not ever able to bring A papers home to their parents...build them up so that they can believe in their own precious worth!!!

CHAPTER 10

How Can I Get Help from My Colleagues?

F ellow music teachers are an obvious source of help for any music teacher. They can share ideas, answer questions, or just serve as a sounding board. They can come watch you teach or let you visit their classroom and see another way of doing things. Of course, many music teachers are alone in their school—or even their district—and must seek support from teachers outside their own school system. Professional organizations and workshops can help. But even if you aren't able to stay in regular contact with other music teachers, you can find help and support from the classroom teachers, administrators, and support staff in your school.

This chapter focuses on the importance of musical and nonmusical colleagues and offers suggestions for building and maintaining healthy relationships with them.

Learn from others.

- I find it extremely important to keep in contact with my fellow colleagues about methods of teaching, musical ideas, and classroom management concepts. It also is an opportunity to bounce new ideas off teachers who have been there.

- I have found that I get a lot of great ideas by sharing with my colleagues. Sometimes when something I'm doing doesn't work, advice from a colleague is worth its weight in gold!

- I find that brainstorming with colleagues in a noncritical environment makes those of us involved even better teachers. Sometimes we gain new ideas or new approaches. Sometimes we just simply receive affirmation for what we already do.

- Meet informally with other music teachers to "shoot the breeze" and get new ideas. Informal contact usually results in a more fluid exchange of ideas!

- I talk with other faculty members. Our music department team (six of us) meets several times a week to plan concerts and fund-raisers and also to let each other know what is going on in our classrooms.

- I keep in touch with the other two elementary music teachers in our system. Working with each other discussing problems or solutions makes me feel less like the Lone Ranger!

- I call friends and pick their brains for new classroom ideas. I use not only all the brains I have, but all I can borrow.

- Talk with other teachers about what works and what doesn't in their own programs. I'm not proud. I will steal anyone's ideas and use them in my program. Why reinvent the wheel!

- I believe it's really important to share great ideas with others. Educators are in the field of sharing knowledge. It shouldn't be limited only to your students! Sharing with colleagues is a lot of fun and is really rewarding when they see you at a later workshop and are excited about using what you shared with them.

- The more I communicate, the more ideas I generate, the more effective I become, and the more willing I am to try out new ideas and concepts. Communicating with colleagues also lets me hear "adult talk," which I sometimes need to hear.

- It's important to know that we're not alone in what we are doing. Our colleagues have valuable ideas to share with us, and we, in turn, have valuable ideas to share with them.

- Watching other teachers, talking to them about what they do, and asking opinions is *the* most helpful aspect of my success and my students' success. Most of my best tricks are from other teachers.

I get so many good ideas from other teachers in our county. We meet monthly during the school year and discuss lessons, project ideas, classroom management, chorus issues, etc. I also meet with our middle-state area teachers and participate with their festivals, offering expanded opportunities for my children.

Our music school has ten teachers on the early childhood faculty. We meet one Friday each month to discuss business (dates, material difficulties, substitutions, etc.), offer each other advice on stressful situations, and share food (a prime ingredient). It is a great time to laugh and cry together over successes and trials.

I don't know where I would be if I didn't have other music teachers around to communicate with. During my first year of teaching, I went to other teachers with every problem, just to make sure I was doing the right thing. Even when I did the wrong things, these teachers were there to share their experiences and wisdom. I learn volumes more from them than I ever did in college methods classes.

As a first-year teacher, I could not have been as successful without a mentor. It was nice to know there was someone there for more ideas, resources, materials, and to talk to about what was going right and what was going wrong. It was also great to get feedback on lessons they observed, and to go observe other teachers to gain even more ideas.

Communicate with mentor-type teachers. I've just completed my first year of teaching high school choral music after teaching middle school for seven previous years. Communicating with colleagues from my home state of Ohio as well as with those here in Georgia helps me to know about new trends and ideas and helps me realize that I really am on track 99 percent of the time. I chat via phone and e-mail quite often with my student-teaching cooperating teacher from twenty years ago and would talk with one of my college professors about strategies and techniques in choral music while he was alive. The neat thing is that I find I have given as much in these relationships as I have received—how incredibly invaluable and rewarding!

- Working in a vacuum is not healthy. Music teachers need opportunities to meet with other teachers in their own specialty.

Be in a mentoring relationship.

- We should all mentor each other and help the newest members with great techniques, ideas, and performance ideas to alleviate burnout.

- As a new teacher, I have learned that veteran teachers have learned a lot from their experience. However, they may take for granted that you know the same things they know and not give you important information. By asking questions you can preempt many mistakes and "oh-I-didn't-know-that" situations.

- Have an effective, successful mentor. Having someone I can really talk to about the frustrations of my job really helps me be a better educator because together we can creatively come up with solutions that I probably couldn't on my own. The other teachers at my school don't teach music, so they don't really understand what it's all about.

- By serving as a mentor for others, I constantly rethink my own methods. I try new things so I can share them with others.

- Share lesson ideas with other teachers. I work closely with the choral educator in my high school, and as a new teacher, I am constantly asking her opinion on whether an idea of mine is valid. Most of the time it is, but she'll let me know if there's a better way to do an activity.

Get involved in professional organizations.

- In most buildings, there is only one music teacher. Interaction with classroom teachers is very helpful, but the "teachers' lounge idea exchange" seldom relates to our discipline. Meetings of professional organizations like MENC and the American Orff-Schulwerk Association help fill this social as well as professional void. Online e-mail lists also help reduce the isolation factor.

- Because I teach college students, keeping in touch with my colleagues through professional journals and organizations helps me keep abreast of new develop-ments in literature for my instrument as well as teaching suggestions from other successful professionals.

A few of the seminars I attended at last year's January convention were absolutely life changing for me and underscored the necessity of interaction with other music teachers. I teach in a private school and direct both the middle school and high school choirs. Our music staff consists of me and the elementary music teacher, so contact with the music educator community is vital!

When I attend our district music educators' meetings and have the opportunity to talk with other elementary music teachers, we share curriculum and assessment plans, ideas for performances, new literature, successes and failures. This is a big help to me since I am the only primary music specialist in my small school district.

- It is too easy to get stuck in your own box and how you do things. Music education is a very isolationist profession, and it's important for us to get a picture of what the rest of the world is like. This can be achieved by attending conferences and reading journal articles, but perhaps more importantly by observing other educators in action and being willing to ask colleagues for help.

- Contact with colleagues is vital to mental health and gaining ideas and support. I am in the midst of an Orff class, and one of the best parts is interacting with others.

- Going to either state or national conventions always makes me feel like there are others out there with a similar situation, and they have great ideas and solutions to problems.

Work together.

- Invite the middle school band director to the elementary school spring concert so he or she can hear strengths and weaknesses and plan for the fall.

- High school teachers must be involved in the lower grades, and teachers in lower grades should remain involved in aspects of the upper school programs.

- I am at the junior high (band). The director at the high school volunteers one or two prep periods each week to come to junior high to work with and get to know students, and I do the same to run sectionals. This keeps us in touch with each other's programs.

- I must recognize that I exist in a program that is the result of effective beginning teaching in my feeder elementaries and that I must continually feed well-prepared students to the high school program my students will be joining. I don't teach or exist as a separate educational entity.

- Visit schools of other levels and interact with teachers of these levels. For example, a college-level music teacher needs to occasionally visit a secondary, middle, or elementary school to observe the younger generations, the music teachers, and the response of the children to the musical experiences. This will reinforce and even change approaches used at the college level.

- Utilize your colleagues. Chorus people should find accompaniments that can use guests from the band and orchestra. This shows everyone playing nicely together.

Observe other teachers—and let them observe you.

- If you have a day off that your colleague doesn't, it wouldn't hurt to go observe a lesson or rehearsal. You might be able to pick up a few tips.

- Observe other music teachers in the classroom. This provides a great forum to learn new teaching methods, to see teaching methods that you don't want to use in your classroom, and to reflect on what you are currently doing in your classroom that is good or bad.

- I continue to observe other teachers, even after twenty years, in order to grow in my own area of expertise.

- Take some time once in a while to observe other teachers, even if it isn't in your subject matter. It is amazing the new techniques and ideas you can add to your repertoire.

- I love to go and watch other successful teachers teach and rehearse. This helps me to fine-tune my skills as a teacher and conductor.

- Have a colleague observe you. It is amazing how helpful it is to have a fellow music teacher watch what you are doing and ask you why.

- Invite other music teachers in to help and listen. It is crucial to get another set of ears into the rehearsal. If you think you can do it all, it really won't happen. Students always react positively to someone who comes in and says the same thing you do day after day.

Build relationships with nonmusic teachers.

- Learn about the other areas in your school. You can't expect support from other faculty if you don't support their efforts.

- Ask colleagues about individual student needs.

- Talk a lot with colleagues—not only music colleagues, but the classroom teachers themselves. It is really important to know what's going on in your kids' lives, especially if there's some trauma.

- Learn alternative strategies from other good teachers. Our resource specialist always helps me learn how to reach those children who have difficulties learning the traditional way.

- Cooperate with fellow teachers. I strive to have the classroom teachers recognize the importance of music education—we are more than just their planning period! I integrate subject matter wherever possible and work on several school committees.

- Work with the regular classroom teachers. Have flexibility if they need the kids for something special.

- Collaborate with staff about curriculum content. Through collaboration, you can gain and provide information, which enhances learning for students. Sometimes these collaborations will result in providing insight and materials for your use or for the classroom teacher's use. The more other staff can count on you, the more respect they have for you and for the music education profession.

> I am able to teach the way I want because I am willing to be extremely flexible with other staff members. For example, I get chairs for concerts set up by P.E. classes because I work with the P.E. teachers instead of bumping heads with them. Other teachers will offer assistance because they know I will work with them when needed.
>
> At my school the classroom teachers make my life easy. If I take a class to perform in the community, we can't perform and return in the thirty minutes of class time. The teachers are great about keeping their class a few extra minutes until I return, or the P.E. teacher takes them with another class so that teacher can have a planning period. I work with a great bunch.
>
> I eat lunch at least once a week in each school (with the teachers whose children I have) so as to connect with them and let them know how their children are doing, invite them personally to concerts, and get feedback and advice on how to deal with a particular child's learning style.
>
> I have found that on the days I eat lunch with other teachers I am more relaxed in the classroom. Something about adult interaction during the day helps. If I stay in my office and just see kids all day I tend to be just like them—unthinking, short-tempered, and easily frustrated.
>
> If I did not have the support of the other teachers, I would be in trouble. They are supportive of what I do and are extremely helpful with whatever I need when it comes to concerts. Whether it is giving me full support and backing for all or part of my program or having the students lined up and getting them on and off stage at the concerts, they are there for me, ready and willing to help.

- Ask teachers what they are doing. Tie in when possible. Offer them suggestions for music they could use in their classrooms to help with subjects they are teaching. Give copies of words when possible to early grades to help encourage reading.

- Work with other teachers, providing music for their class plays and other programs; organize a district or school teachers' chorus or band; invite classroom teachers or student teachers to observe music classes.

- Occasionally socialize in the lounge. At first it seemed like a big waste of time to socialize in the lounge, but now I have found that is part of how you make and maintain relationships that are necessary to keep a school working.

- Always maintain good faculty relationships. If you do not have a good working relationship with the classroom teachers, they can make your attempts at teaching a nightmare. They may dissuade a marginal academic child from signing up to play, they may not allow children to leave their classrooms for lessons, and they may schedule major activities against your performance schedule.

- I am always explaining to a regular classroom teacher the importance of music, what content I teach in my classroom, how it helps their reading goals, the movement aspect, etc. Some teachers really don't understand that I have a packed curriculum on my own and don't just teach silly songs and games in general music.

- Communication between staff members at a school is crucial. At my elementary school, the teachers are flexible enough to give me pull-out time because I work hard at those relationships.

- Music teachers are not the only ones to talk to. We need to get to know all of the teachers in our buildings and draw from their experience and expertise.

Keep lines of communication open.

- I try hard to let our school know about what we are doing. I do this with announcements (during the daily morning announcements), talking with other teachers, and posting band information throughout the school.

- Communicate with fellow teachers who are involved and affected by your activities and schedules. They will appreciate your time and trouble to make them feel important as well.

- Keep staff informed of upcoming events—how programs will impact schedules, who will be involved, where events will take place, specifics (with diagrams) of assigned placement and entry patterns, special assignments for a class or a student or group of students, the order of the program. Repeat communication with additional details as preparation progresses.

- I've found the other teachers and school staff to be more flexible and supportive

if I keep them involved in decisions concerning dates, times, and even subjects of the songs studied.

- Always, always, always let administrators, secretaries, teachers, custodians, and cafeteria workers know about *anything* that may require extra time from students or any change to a schedule. Always thank them at every performance.

- I regularly send out a newsletter to all the staff and administration on the progress and events of the music department.

Be involved in your school.

- It is important to be a part of your school, not only as the music teacher but as a teacher. Be on something like your staff development committee or the teachers' association. Be an integral part of your school.

- Be part of your staff. Speak out at staff meetings, volunteer for committees, and be active in your teachers' association.

- Be a team player in a faculty. I have two schools, so integrating myself into the faculties is not always easy. But putting myself on the treat-bringing schedule, being at faculty meetings, and communicating with the classroom teachers at my schools is crucial to the attitude the children bring to the music room.

- Involvement in the school's vision team or advisory committee helps me connect what I do in the classroom to the mission of the school. It also makes my program and its value very obvious to all stakeholders.

Keep administrators on your side.

- Have a close relationship with administration. The closer the communication with administration, the better you understand the needs within the community.

- Keep administrators happy...find out what they're looking for and give them more.

HALLE DINKLE   BY TOM BATIUK

Have non-work-related conversations. Ask, "'How's the family?" (and really care) from time to time.

Don't forget support staff.

- Coordinate with the media person and the computer lab person.

- Remember that the custodians and secretaries are your best friends.

- Enlist the support of the custodian. I cannot begin to list the number of times that the school custodian or the school secretary has come to the rescue. They are invaluable to any and all programs. Support them and always demonstrate your appreciation. (Have a few of your students play or sing for their birthday.)

- Getting along with the janitor saves hours of time. She helps move chairs, tighten stands, even work on props.

How Can I Build Community Support?

P arents and community members can do a lot to help or hinder a music program. Parents bring their children to concerts, help prepare for special events, and make sure their children are practicing at home. Community members can drum up enthusiasm for a program and even provide financial support. But parents and community members need something from you if they are going to support your programs. They need to know what is going on, what your needs are, and why the music program is important.

This chapter provides some suggestions for getting parents and the community more involved in the music program.

Communicate with parents.

- Communicate with families. Parents and families are essential to the development of a child. To join with the families in the development of a child will be rewarding for everyone involved. Communication with families will also

> I have found that using the Internet and e-mail is very beneficial in communicating with students, parents, teachers, and administrators. I realize that memos don't always make it home, so I e-mail information to parents and students. I have also set up a Web page with all of our performance dates, quiz material, and other information. This has helped keep parents up-to-date.
>
> I have experimented with many different means of communication and have found that a monthly newsletter mailed to the home is the best way of keeping parents informed about the happenings and classwork of the program. Syllabi at the beginning of the semester along with a calendar of events is also a vital part of this communication. I am currently working on a Web site that will serve as an additional means of communication for me.

I have developed a newsletter that is distributed quarterly. The past two years I have distributed it to the households of my students. I have also sent it to step-families of students. This ensures that concert dates, outstanding achievements, and regular classroom news make it home. High school students don't always take information home to Mom and Dad in the most efficient manner. This year I plan to distribute it to the entire school district faculty and staff—including administrators, secretarial staff, custodial staff, and our food service.

parents concerning classroom activities, special events, etc. Provide articles and photographs to local newspapers relating to special activities and events.

- We use meetings, voice mail bulletins, Web site technology, phone calls, mailings, and e-mail to communicate with staff, students, and parents.

- Crank up the public relations for school concerts, and make certain that parents and other stakeholders know the successes of you and your students.

- Plan for and provide regular newsletters to students, parents, and community leaders that outline group activities, student achievement, awards, and performance schedules.

- The music program is often the PR for the school. Sometimes it is the only opportunity for the community to find out how terrific young people can be. The community is the ultimate "controller" of whether or not music remains in school.

- Educate and share experiences with the community. Share current music research with parents and audiences. This is vital to our support of music programs now and in the future.

- Every program, whether an established one or one in its infancy, has a responsibility to its constituents to create an impact in the community. I've found that in having a program with a high profile, students, fellow staff, and parents are more eager to actively support in a variety of ways.

HALLE DINKLE   BY TOM BATIUK

- The only way we can help the community see the importance of arts education is to become our own promoters—we have to be good at public relations. Get to know your newspaper and television people.

- Constantly promote music education. I shout how good my kids are at every possible moment. My boosters do the same. We make sure publicity is in the newspaper every week about some aspect of the music program.

- Communicate with others. Let the community and other educators know what is happening. Never be afraid to toot your own horn. Let the word around town start with you so you can be sure it is a good word.

There is virtually no budget for my music program. I am mostly funded by donated money from the community, which comes primarily in the form of collections taken at concerts. We do approximately five concerts per semester, and my program runs in the black each year as a result. I have also had several thousand dollars donated for the purpose of purchasing a new sound system after my old one went out during a concert!

I try to include parents, faculty, and community members in concert activities. This year, our community group made a video to be submitted for the World's Largest Concert, and that same group—along with my fourth-, fifth- and sixth-grade students—produced a "canned food concert" to raise food for our local food bank.

Our elementary choir students performed a spring concert and enjoyed an ice cream supper with family and faculty. Each student created a ceramic dish for the event. Everyone enjoyed the evening.

Perform, perform, perform.

- We can't expect the support of the community if they don't see the program.

- Bring more music to the public. In addition to, or instead of, two large concerts a year, do some "mini" performances for parents and the general public. The parents will be more willing to support and aid the teacher when their child is really able to be seen and heard in a small group. Parents and grandparents want to know what their children are being taught, so here is the chance to make music a total part of curriculum.

- Music can be a blessing for any community, and it is our privilege to be in a position to bring that to the people. Music draws people together and stirs emotions. We music educators, by sharing our talents, can give the gifts of music to our neighbors.

- The only way that we can be assured that people in the community know what we're doing is to be out there. If you're invited to perform in the local festival, go! Invite the public to hear your concerts. The community needs to know what we're doing so that they understand what a vital part music plays in the lives of our children.

- Getting out into the community is perhaps the most direct way for music directors to receive the recognition, respect, and support they deserve for themselves and for their music programs. Taking performing groups out of the school building also keeps the students motivated to perform their best. Place music articles in the PTA newsletters. Have students perform at PTA/school board meetings, as the music director explains the music program to parents and administrators. Publish weekly articles about the music program in the local newspaper. Send complimentary concert tickets (even if the concerts are free) to local businesses, retirement communities, and town council members.

Take your ensembles into the community.

- We have several community groups that invite our choirs to come and perform for them on a regular basis. This not only supplies great music for the community, but it also gives the students a sense of purpose.

- One of the most important things you can do is to get out into the community with your groups. We are always trying to *sell the program* to others. Playing demonstration concerts at your feeder schools is invaluable. Let them know about all of your program, not just one group or style of music.

- Get the community excited about your program. It is easier to ask for support for your groups if you have gone out and supported community events. The town parade, the special ceremony at city hall, and performances at the elder care center are all important events for getting the music group a good name. You might view it as less important than festival, but these events will get support in the community.

After each concert, Holiday and Spring, I take the chorus and band students to the local hospital and nursing homes to perform for the residents. It is *great* PR.

Our performing ensembles get out into the community often. The holiday ensemble performs for the tree-lighting service every December. The community provides hot chocolate and cookies after the service. Community and students come together...what an education in itself!

I teach in an area of South Florida that is "yuppie" but also "very retired." My show choir goes out into the community a great deal during the school year, and my students know they are out there to spread the word about what is good about public education and young people. This is an important mission for our school and helps promote understanding within the older population.

- Taking my students to perform in the community naturally compels me to have my students performing at their best. I am more aware of how I spend rehearsal time, and I want to be more effective as a choral director and teacher so my students are at their best.

- Getting out into the community is so important. We had a unique opportunity this year, when my advanced (seventh- and eighth-grade) chorus sang as part of a cantorial concert at a local temple. It's important to balance these performances. I could take my groups out once a week if I wanted to, but there's more to chorus than performing the music that goes over well at community performances.

I enjoy great support from my parent community, and I believe this is in part due to the fact that I make an effort to communicate to them the process of musical skill development and how our activities develop these skills. I believe this is especially important to parents who have had very little musical experience.

I took a course at ABC (American Band College) in 1998 in music advocacy that has tremendously influenced this aspect of my professional practice. Since I took that course, I have become an active advocate in my school district and state for the benefits of music education in the lives of the students I teach. I don't think our programs will ever be *overfunded* and our profession given *too much respect*, so I believe music advocacy is necessary to get the word out about the benefits of what we do for students.

Be an advocate for music.

- Support from many different stakeholders is necessary for music teachers to be successful. They range from parents to faculty, administrators, school board members, business, media, and our own music colleagues. Whether it is promotional or financial in nature, support is necessary for success.

- Keep informed about the latest developments in music research and the importance of music education in the lives of students and the community.

- Articulate your philosophy of music education. Begin with the end in mind, and be able to identify the values and purpose of an education in music. Be pre-

The following publications from MENC can help you in your efforts to educate others about the value of music education:

• *The Benefits of the Study of Music: Why We Need Music Education in Our Schools*, 2002, is a brochure filled with quotes and statistics about the value of music.

• *The Music Education Advocate's Toolkit*, 2001, contains tools that can help you build support for your program.

• *Music Makes the Difference: Music, Brain Development, and Learning*, 2000, includes articles on the links between music and other learning as well as discussion of the intrinsic value of music.

Visit http://www.supportmusic.com and http://www.musicfriends.org for more resources that can help you be an effective music education advocate.

pared to talk and write about why it is important to study music—describe it in words that you can use with parents, other teachers, administrators, and school board members.

- Speak up on matters that concern your program. People will not look after a music program on your behalf. You have to fight for every scrap of support that you can get in a world that is dominated by sports.

- Keep up on brain research. Try to keep administrators aware of the importance of music and fine arts in the total development of the brain.

- I like students and administrators to understand that music has a crucial role in the atmosphere of education. Academics understandably are the most important part. Athletics are also vital to a school's spirit. Music is the soul that gives the emotion to a school. With only a brain and a heart we aren't much! Thank God we as music educators can give education its soul.

Ask for help.

- Giving parents a stake in the music program and allowing them to be involved in classroom activities and programs not only helps me to delegate some details to volunteers, it also brings about a positive response to the music program.

MENC's *Music Booster Manual* (1989) provides information on starting and managing a local booster organization. You can read an excerpt at http://www.musicfriends.org/booster.html.

- Use parents in site-based teams to keep them informed. These teams need to be used at all levels and not just at the high school levels in the form of booster clubs.

- Seek extra money for advisors. If you want a marching band—you need marching instructors. Show choir—need special instructors. These folks cost money and somehow need to be covered by the school site.

HALLE DINKLE   BY TOM BATIUK

 By applying for the Arts in Education grants, I keep myself abreast of new ideas and methods. This past year our school was granted ten thousand dollars for vocal pedagogy. We brought in area specialists monthly and were able to take the students out into the surrounding area to experience choral music up close and personal. We did regular assessments, and students grew in knowledge and confidence. It really made a difference in their performances.

Have a strong parent booster group. The laws in Washington State governing ASB monies are getting so restrictive, I rely heavily on my boosters for running fund-raisers and providing support financially that I don't get from the district. This past year, my boosters purchased new concert uniforms for the entire band and financed half of our trip to southern California.

I maintain a friendship with my local music store. I cannot possibly listen to every demo disk that comes in. And I cannot possibly review every piece of new literature. It is the advice, not to mention the camaraderie, that I have developed with this music dealer that keeps me informed on the newest literature and band technique books.

The more you can involve a whole family in music, the more support you will have. Pep band used to be a great challenge when all of my best musicians were playing ball. When we watered down arrangements and invited community people to play, we could make it work. We also have Buccaneer Band Buddies. They are little brothers and sisters or younger students, some in beginning band and some pre-band-aged, who come and sit with the pep band as their buddy. They cheer, clap along to the beat, sing along, and have a great time. Everyone loves it. The more people in a family that are involved, the more support we get for our program.

- Ask for money for materials. Our school site does not consider the music literature I purchase to be my textbooks. Therefore my six-hundred-dollar-a-year budget has to cover all music purchases. Music materials should be considered our textbooks and be funded accordingly.

- Draw upon the expertise of folk in the community. Use senior citizens who remember songs and stories from their own early childhood.

- Maintain a good relationship with the instrument repair dealers. These are the people who will make or break your program. They will rent good instruments to your students or junk. They will take good care of your needs, or do the minimum to keep your business.

- Don't be afraid to ask for parents to come in and help out with fitting uniforms and other "detail" tasks that can be very time-consuming when you try to do everything yourself. Communicate to parents exactly what your expectations are, and you will have more involved parents.

APPENDIX

MENC Survey Results

I n 2001, MENC: The National Association of Music Education asked its members to participate in an online survey titled, "What Are the Essential Practices of Music Teachers?" Teachers were asked to rank a variety of practices and list their top five practices and provide explanations or anecdotes related to those practices. The complete questions used on the survey and the results are described below.

What are the essential practices of successful music educators?

We're interested in collecting (and possibly disseminating) information on this topic. By submitting your viewpoints here, you give MENC permission to use your words in public dissemination, either electronically or via published hard copy.

According to Webster's 9th New Collegiate Dictionary:

practice:
actual performance or application; a repeated or customary action; the usual way of doing something; a systematic exercise for proficiency; the condition of being proficient through systematic exercise

1. Please rank the following practices according to their importance to your effectiveness as a music educator. Using a scale of 1–5: 1–extremely important, 2–very important, 3–important, 4–slightly important, 5–not so important

Survey results are listed after each question, beginning with the rankings from 1 to 5 and followed by the number of teachers selecting that ranking.

Communicating with colleagues (examples: reading professional journals, attending meetings, helping other teachers with adjudication, talking to colleagues in music and in other disciplines about professional concerns, writing or participating actively in print or online exchanges)

1: 445   2: 204   3: 96   4: 50   5: 65

Maintaining personal balance (examples: keeping fit and active in areas outside of the profession)

| 1: 336 | 2: 264 | 3: 154 | 4: 56 | 5: 50 |

Keeping up your chops (example: continuing to practice, study, and perform the music you love, and/or new musical avenues)

| 1: 279 | 2: 289 | 3: 180 | 4: 68 | 5: 43 |

Getting to the subject (example: using well-thought out pedagogical techniques to help the students gain skill and knowledge in music)

| 1: 498 | 2: 192 | 3: 47 | 4 : 39 | 5 : 81 |

Keeping the kids in line (example: developing and using consistent, effective motivation and discipline to keep the students on-task and learning)

| 1: 505 | 2: 186 | 3: 47 | 4: 43 | 5: 78 |

Improvising and composing (In the classroom, that is: creating and evaluating new methods of presenting material to the students)

| 1: 250 | 2: 276 | 3: 186 | 4: 89 | 5: 51 |

Filling and filing (Maintaining clear records on student progress, program finances, and the other details that you have to track)

| 1: 212 | 2: 288 | 3: 242 | 4: 76 | 5: 42 |

Getting out into the community (Cranking up the public relations for school concerts and making certain that parents and other stakeholders know the successes of you and your students)

| 1: 325 | 2: 286 | 3: 121 | 4: 62 | 5: 61 |

2. **Now, please list five top practices which help you to be a better teacher. You are not limited to those practices listed in item 1 above. Feel free to give an explanation or anecdote to illustrate your choices in the text box below.**

The practices and stories included in the book are a sampling of the many responses teachers provided in this section of the survey. The following are the top twenty-five practices that teachers named in this section followed by the number of teachers who listed that practice.

Relationships with students	121
Enthusiasm and sense of fun	75
Professional development	68
High standards for students	64
Preparation and planning for class	58

Literature/repertoire	54
Open to suggestions from students and colleagues	44
Assessment of students	40
Interdisciplinary collaboration with other teachers	38
Sense of humor	36
Goal setting for self and students	34
Use of technology	33
Creating of performance opportunities for students	32
Teaching basic concepts of music reading and composition	29
Staying current with new pedagogy techniques	28
Observing and being observed by other teachers	28
Passion for teaching and/or music	28
Variety in teaching style	25
Individual time with each student	26
Flexibility with unexpected changes	24
Sequential curriculum	24
Respect for students	21
Being a role model for students	21
Self-reflection/assessment	21
Musical experiences outside class	20

3. Please indicate at what grade levels you teach (check all that apply):

Pre K:	67
Kindergarten:	229
Elementary:	468
Middle (6–8):	416
High School (9–12):	302
College Level:	101
Post graduate :	21

4. Please indicate what subject areas you teach (check all that apply):

Band:	362
String/orchestra:	114
Chorus (all vocal groups):	399
Jazz:	167
Conducting:	46
Theory:	37
Composition:	61
General music:	510
Other:	167

Contributors

The following teachers are among the over 850 teachers who participated in the MENC Essential Practices Survey. Because participants were not required to provide identifying information, we cannot list the names of everyone who participated. However, MENC does greatly appreciate the time that each music educator involved in this survey took to share ideas. Whether their names are listed below and whether their comments are reproduced in this book, we thank all participants for their willingness to share their wisdom.

Diane M. Abrams
Brooke Adams
Ed Adams
Fran Addicott
Ellen Baer
Michael Baer
Kelly Ballard
Matt Barkley
Bill Bartman
Richard Bateman
Julie Beard
Jennifer Beimborn
Donald Bell
Tony Bernard
Kelly Jo Birmingham
Jayme M. Bishop
Michelle Blassengale
Michael Blostein
Wendy Borst
Karen Bradley
Brenda Bressler
Jan Brewer
Charles Brodie
Kristy Broers
Cynthia A. Brown
Della Brown
Elizabeth Brown
Kathy Brown
Cecilia Bullough
Lovina Bundy
Carolyn Burns

Nicole Byrd-Phelps
Ruth Calcaterra
Rob Caldwell
Stephen Cassola
Jim Chesebrough
Dean Chiapetto
Shannon Cholewa
Greg Cissell
Christy Cook
Sandra Cox
Sandra Crocker
Amy Crosby
Neil Crotty
Beth Cummings
Mark A. D'Angelo
Marilyn Davidson
Lisa S. Davis
Jo Lynn DeGolia
Bruce Deisinger
Catherine DeLanoy
Helen Demong
Valerie DePriest
Darlene Duke
Stephanie Dupuis
David DeStefano
Christopher DeWilde
Ashley Dougan
Thomas Douglass
Michael M. Dragen
Bill Dugger
Rick Dugger

Darlene Duke
Christine Dunleavy
Stephanie Dupuis
Mary Estell
Debbie Fahmie
Douglas A. Farr
Kim Farrell
Amy Finnerty
Fred Forsh
Amanda Freese
Lynnda Fuller
Ronnie Gaddis
Cheryl Gapinski
Trisha Garnes
Doris Gazda
Rita Germer
Joanne Gilbert
Laurie Gilbreath
Bonnie Glazier
Chris Glenn
James A. Goodman
Monica J. Gould
Sandra Greene
Jan Greisch
Karen Griebel
Joy Grimsley
Keith Haan
Rebecca Hall
Christeen Hampton
Laura Hanlon
Chris Hansen

Angela Harman
Dorlene Harris
Judy Hartwig
Juliette Hawk
Tom Hay
D.R. Henke
Jayne Herman
Sister Mary Hilary, O.P.
Robert D. Holland
Richard Holsomback
Laura Horst
Elise Howell
Linda Huck
William L. Humphrey
Kara Hunnicutt
Jeanne Hutto
Jan Hyatt
Althea Jerome
Kevin Johnson
Nancy Jolley
Betty Sue Kitchen
Jane Koch
Anna-Marie Koszarycz
Deb Knisely
Jamie Koroch
Larry Krauser
Stephanie Ladlie
Erik Larson
Terry Laubscher
John Lester
Eric Lewis
Wilbur W. Lewis
Lisa Lichter
Jessica Lichty
Michael Lisi
Anne Littleton
Julie Longfield
D. Scott Loose
Margaret K. Love
Rosemary Lubbers
Rich Lundahl
Steven Lyons
Kenneth Mackie
Ralph Maddox
Joyce Magann
Jill Mahoney
Sara Maloney
Ed Martin
Gordon A. Martinez
Lewis May
Lyle McCaslin
Kevin J. McDonald
Lyn McKay

Sue McKenzie
Sheila Mendel
Phyllis Mentzos
Chris Metcalfe
Norma Meyer
Nancy Middlemas
R. Clair Miller
Christopher Minarich
Sheri Mitchell
Tom Mitchell
Kevin Mixon
Charlotte Mizener
Patty Moffett
Debra W. Moore
Silvia Moore-Young
Judith Murphy
Luanne Murphy
Carol Myers
Jill Nedorostek
Michael D. Neller
Al Newman
Scott C. Niehoff
Denese Odegaard
Michael Oglesby
Jendean Olson
Judy Olson
Marianne Oltmann
Robert Oswren
Michael Palumbo
Loius Pape
Betty Neill G. Parsons
Denise Pearson
Kirstin S. Peltz
Lynn Pernezny
Katie Peterson
Carol Petrucci
Reta R. Phifer
Ken Quehrn
Karen E. Randall
Thomas B. Raphael
Jay Regan
Amy F. Richter
Katy Ries
Gary Ross
Dr. Clark Roush
David M. Royse
Randall Royer
Kathy Rutherford
Vicki Salmon
Barbara Sanders
Dana Scaglione
Molly Schaeren
Naomi Schick

Lynne Secrist
Charles Sedgwick
Judy P. Shoemaker
Christin Simon
William Slechta
John Stanley
Stephanie Standerfer
Tim Stephan
Michele Steiner
Barb Stevanson
Pamela Stover
Bob Straka
Michael Stratechuk
Barbara Swigart
Richard Tengowski
Roger Thaden
Kimberly G. Thompson
Phyllis Timko
Rebecca Timmons
Pat Toben
Angee Tonsmeire
Karen Townsend
Scott Trach
Sara C. Trotman
Larry Trujillo
Annette B. Tuten
William C. Ulrickson
Heather Van Dyke
Rollin Varness
Donna Vojcsik
Terry Vonderheide
Richard A. Waggoner
Karen Walker
Barbara Walston
Laura Weaver
Terry Weber
Leslie Webster
Alice Wells
Amy Werdin
Kayla Werlin
Brent White
Nancy Wildoner
Brenda Williams
Karen Williams
Philip C. Williams
Renee Wilson-Wicker
Pamela J. Winkler
Elaine Wischmeier
Doug Wood
Linda Wood
Jay Wucher
Robin York
Frank Zahn